CRAZY
LITTLE THING
CALLED
MARRIAGE

Crazy
Little Thing
Called
Marriage 200655

12 Secrets
for a Lifelong
Romance

DR. GREG & ERIN SMALLEY

FOREWORD BY GARY CHAPMAN

 TYNDALE HOUSE PUBLISHERS, INC.
CAROL STREAM, ILLINOIS

In memory of the late S. Truett Cathy
and his bride of sixty-seven years, Jeannette
McNeil Cathy. A marriage well done.

Contents

Foreword

Every married person naturally wants a thriving marriage. Every spouse wants peace and harmony in the home. Every reasonable husband wants to feel he's meeting his wife's needs. And every good wife wants to feel the same toward her husband.

That's why the habits we form in marriage are so important. As we look at a situation, especially if we're unhappy or there's open conflict, what are our first thoughts? What assumptions do we make about our spouse's motives? What words flow from our mouths, perhaps before we've even considered what we ought to say?

Sadly, it's all too easy to get off track. The train can jump the rails before we realize what has happened. How well I remember a time when that occurred in my own marriage! Though I've told the story before, it bears repeating here.

My wife, Karolyn, and I were having a typically hectic weekday morning, getting the kids ready for school and me ready to go to work. Searching frantically, I asked her, "Karolyn, where is my briefcase?"

"I don't know," she answered.

I take my briefcase home every night, and I leave it in the same place. Since it wasn't there now, she had to have moved it.

"Come on, Karolyn," I said, raising the volume. "I'm in a hurry! Where is my briefcase? I put it right in there by the dresser last night, and it's gone. Where did you put it?"

The reply came back—also at higher volume—"Gary, I don't know where your briefcase is!"

We went back and forth like this a couple of more times, each time a little louder. I was getting really upset. Of course she had moved my briefcase, but for whatever reason she couldn't or wouldn't say where. Didn't she understand how much I needed it and how big a hurry I was in? Didn't she care how frustrated I was becoming?

Burning with anger, I sped the kids out the door, into the car, and off to school. I cooled down enough to speak calmly to them about their schoolwork. But after they were on their way into the building, I immediately went back to full-burn anger with Karolyn for losing my case.

For the entire drive to my office, my thoughts steamed along like this: *How could I have married such a scatterbrain? My briefcase is important. In fact, I can't operate without it. What am I going to do today?*

You can see all the assumptions I was making, right? And from them I had drawn conclusions, none of them complimentary to the love of my life. But her unwillingness to help was driving me crazy.

As ideas and emotions like these churned in my mind and my stomach, I parked the car and stomped into the office. And what did I see the moment I set foot through the door? My briefcase, of course, exactly where I had set it down the night before.

I'm happy to report the story gets better from there. All that building anger instantly drained from my mind and body. In its place sprang up embarrassment, chagrin, and a desire to make things right. How could I have entertained such thoughts about Karolyn? How could I have said such words to her, and in such a tone of voice?

Being human, I briefly wondered if I could somehow explain away my unkind and unloving words and behavior. But no, there was only one acceptable course of action. First, I prayed and asked God to forgive me. I thanked Him for the Cross and the assurance that my sins have, indeed, been paid for. My conscience clear toward Him, I then asked for the grace and strength to do the next thing necessary.

I picked up the phone, called Karolyn, told her what she already knew, made my apology, and asked for *her* forgiveness.

And how did she respond? "I thought you'd call!"

Clearly, some of my habits relative to our marriage still needed work. But she also knew that one of my better habits was and is a shared commitment not to let disputes fester and anger to take hold. She understood I would soon realize my mistake, admit my fault, and take steps to set things right between us.

Like any other good habits, however, healthy habits in marriage develop only when you're intentional about them and put consistent effort into growing them in place of bad habits. Our human nature tends toward laziness and self-centeredness—neither of which produces strong relationships, let alone a thriving marriage.

That's why I'm so excited to recommend to you the book you now hold in your hands, *Crazy Little Thing Called Marriage*. Greg and Erin Smalley have looked carefully at the best research about how to have a great marriage. In addition, they've drawn on their own extensive experience in helping to heal marriages that had stood on the brink of collapse.

From this research and experience, they have identified twelve traits, or "romance secrets," of a thriving marriage.

They've seen that if you learn these traits and grow these habits of thought and action, you, too, can have a great marriage.

At the very heart of what makes marriage work is "this thing called love." God loved us when we were very unlovely. When we respond to His love and receive what Christ did for us, His love begins to flow through us. But it flows only as we maintain a close relationship with Him. As I said before, by nature we are not lovers but self-centered and selfish. Two consistently selfish people will never have a healthy marriage. Two lovers, on the other hand, will experience all that God had in mind when He created us male and female.

So enjoy reading this book. Learn the twelve habits that allow you to cooperate with God in keeping love alive in your marriage. The practical ideas the Smalleys share will encourage and equip those couples who want to experience a thriving marriage.

Gary Chapman

PhD, author of The Five Love Languages

THIS THING CALLED LOVE

Three things will last forever—faith, hope,
and love—and the greatest of these is love.
—1 Corinthians 13:13, NLT

Not long ago, my fifteen-year-old son, Garrison, held up a VHS tape he'd found in the closet. "My history teacher showed us pictures of these the other day," he joked. "I didn't know that any had survived."

This comment resulted in the idea to digitize. The decades-old tape was of a wedding ceremony, specifically the nuptials of one love-struck Gregory Thomas Smalley to the beautiful Erin Christine Murphy. Since we hadn't owned a VCR player for many years, I decided it was time to convert it to a DVD.

In many ways it felt like yesterday—watching Erin, escorted by her parents, walk down the aisle to my waiting hand. In other ways, our wedding felt like a lifetime ago. I don't mean that as in "the ol' ball and chain," because I love my wife and our marriage. But it was strange to see my twenty-three-year-old self. I was barely shaving, and yet there I stood, pledging life-changing vows.

> I, Greg, take you, Erin, to be my wife, to have and to hold from this day forward, for better or for worse, for richer, for poorer, in sickness and in health, to love and to cherish, until death do us part.

And that's when I noticed something remarkable. I replayed the scene several times to make sure I'd heard it correctly. I smiled at the realization that everything I've learned about marriage in the past twenty-four years—both as a husband and as a psychologist—could be summed up in two simple words. And yet I'd failed to grasp their significance when I'd said them.

What are these life-changing words? *To love.*

I'm sure you're thinking, *Love? That's it—that's your big revelation about the secret for a great marriage? I want my money back!*

But hold on—I know that you recognize the importance of love. In fact, a recent Pew Research Center survey showed that 88 percent of Americans cited love as a "very important" reason to get married, ahead of lifelong commitment (81 percent) and companionship (76 percent).[1] But I'm not talking about love, the noun. My moment of revelation was hearing my very own lips vow "to love" Erin.

Eighty-eight percent of Americans cited love as a "very important" reason to get married.

This short phrase is the secret of a thriving marriage and the foundation of everything that you'll learn within the pages of this book.

And the twelve secrets to lifelong romance, based on biblical concepts of how "to love," will rock your marriage boat because the culture has been broadcasting love lies.

Society's views on love and marriage are not only false, but they can also severely harm or handicap your relationship. The toxic parts of unbiblical ideas about love are often rooted deep in the heart. Maxims such as, "Your spouse will 'complete' you," sound great as a headline, but over time false ideas result in emotional pain and relationship strain.

Let me tell you a story to show what I mean.

TEAM SMALLEY

Erin and I developed this material together, working side by side as marriage partners and counselors. It represents ideas that have been forming for two decades during the presentation of more than two hundred marriage workshops together.

For the sake of readability, the bulk of the material is written from my perspective. Erin will add her feminine angle whenever she has a particular encouragement for women (or whenever I, being encumbered by my masculinity, can't effectively articulate the fairer sex's viewpoint).

LOVE'S FINE PRINT

I'll never forget a special phone call I made to Erin during our engagement. I was euphoric about a fortuitous turn of events.

After she answered the phone, I asked her to sit down and brace herself, then I proudly announced that I had received official notification in the mail that *I had won the big sweepstakes!* Yes, indeed, Erin was preparing to marry a *very* rich man. I was in the running for a new car, a free luxury trip, or even one million dollars!

At first Erin was speechless. I thought this would truly be any bride's dream come true: entering marriage with no financial worries. So it was no wonder the glorious news had stunned her into silence. A minute later I didn't understand when she actually laughed out loud while I went on and on about how we would spend the money and what I was going to buy her.

One is very crazy when in love.

Sigmund Freud, founder of psychoanalysis

To make a long and embarrassing story short, I had fallen for a scam. (Today Erin says that when she was in nursing school, she'd had conversations that were eerily similar—with the patients in the hospital's psychiatric ward.)

Indeed these marketers had done a great job presenting their pitch. I wasn't able to distinguish between reality and the hope of financial independence. The "winner" notification sounded legitimate with all the right legal jargon. The stationery looked so authentic—the envelope even had a wax seal!

I felt humiliated. Not only had I believed I was a millionaire, I had also told my entire family and bragged to many of my graduate school friends.

In one day I learned that without reading and understanding the fine print, I could easily end up sounding like a fool.

When it comes to marriage, we are being scammed as well. However, it's not by some crook peddling a bogus sweepstakes;

it's by the culture that we live in. We are being sold ideas about marriage that contain "fine print," which sets up couples—even couples who have been married ten years or longer—to fail.

THE LOVE LIES

See if you recognize some of these popular marriage scams:

Marriage is easy when you find "the one."

Conflict is a sign of a troubled relationship.

Romance and passion will always be alive in a good marriage.

Your spouse should automatically know what you need.

Marriage is about being happy.

Spouses will naturally grow closer as time goes by.

Love is self-sustaining.

Oneness is about losing your identity.

Differences are the problem in most marriages.

As wonderful as they sound, these faulty beliefs create unrealistic expectations that in general undermine your marriage relationship. But I want to focus on one myth in particular. In my opinion, it's the most destructive. This concept is best summed up by French novelist George Sand writing to future daughter-in-law Lina Calamatta about marriage: "There is only one happiness in this life, to love and be loved."[2]

As I have already pointed out, this quote contains a kernel of truth. It is good "to love." The distorted mush is the "be loved" part. Happiness is not dependent on finding someone to love you. The popular notion that we *need* to be loved by our spouse, or anyone for that matter, is intellectual swill.

The truth is that I don't *need* Erin to love me.

I know this sounds counterintuitive and crazy—because we've all probably been bombarded with this cultural lie through magazine articles, movie scripts, and music lyrics. One song recorded by country music artist Wynonna Judd offers this advice, "You got to find somebody to love you / Someone to be there for you night and day."[3]

The Bible, however, doesn't say that you need to find someone to love you.

Let that sink in. *You don't need to find someone to love you.*

There's nothing in Scripture that says this. Not. One. Verse.

You don't need your spouse to love you, but you do need love. *You need God's love.*

God *is* love (1 John 4:8), and His love is perfect, everlasting,

---

WHEN A MARRIAGE IS UNSAFE

The scope of this book is not intended to address a marriage broken down by physical violence, sexual exploitation, or psychological abuse. Do you think you are in an emotionally hurtful or a violence-filled relationship? Do you believe your spouse is emotionally unstable and could harm you or him/herself? If so, one or both of you could be in danger. If you are in a life-threatening situation, dial 911. For non-immediate help, we invite you to call 1-800-A-Family (1-800-232-6459) between 6 a.m. and 8 p.m. Mountain Time. It may take as long as forty-eight hours for a qualified, licensed counselor to return your call, so please leave a message with your contact information.

Focus on the Family counselors can support you as you take action to ensure your safety and the safety of your loved ones. You will also find assistance in locating Christian resources in your area for ongoing care.

unconditional, sacrificial, steadfast, faithful, genuine, and active. Your need to be loved has been completely met by God.

The culture doesn't acknowledge that a personal, loving God exists. So it sells you this lie, and it's a whopper:

> If you fail to find your "soul mate," then a massive "love hole" will remain in your heart, and you will spend the rest of your meaningless life weeping and gnashing your teeth until you find someone else who will give you the love that you so crave.

THE LOVE TRUTH

Here's a summary of the love truth found in Scripture:

> You don't have a "love hole" in your heart. God is the source of love. Your need to be loved has already been 100 percent satisfied by your heavenly Father.

Your spouse will never be "the source" of love in your life. This is God's exclusive role—and He is a jealous lover! We are constantly reminded of God's possessive love throughout the Bible: "I have loved you with an everlasting love" (Jeremiah 31:3, ESV). The apostle Paul called us "dearly loved children" (Ephesians 5:1) and John wrote, "Beloved, if God so loved us, we also ought to love one another" (1 John 4:11, ESV). The word *beloved* means "much loved." The Creator of the universe loves you completely!

So, our first and most important job in marriage is to open our hearts to God's unlimited love. This is why the greatest commandment begins with an instruction to love God: "Love the Lord your God with all your heart and with all your soul and with all your mind and with all your strength" (Mark 12:30).

When you put God first, He promises to meet all your needs. "Seek the Kingdom of God above all else, and live righteously, and he will give you everything you need" (Matthew 6:33, NLT). God alone can fill you to the full.

Nothing on this earth compares to being loved by Him (Ephesians 3:16-21).

Then Why Marriage?

God designed marriage to start with His love. The Lord created you to depend completely upon Him—heart, soul, mind, and strength. He fills you up in ways that nothing else can. You will never find ultimate satisfaction except in a vital, dynamic relationship with God.

That being said, God's design for us includes community—both a blood community and a faith community. Marriage is God's plan for individuals and also for community. God gave us marriage as a gift, but that gift does not supersede our primary relationship, which is with Him as our Source of life and love.

To Love . . .

Once you are able to receive God's love, as a married person you have a job to do. Freed from the bonds of trying to get your spouse to love you, you are now able to love fully. Instead of spending time, effort, and energy on looking inward, your job is to look outward and love your spouse.

Erase the cultural scams and myths about matrimony from your mind and heart; this is the real job your heavenly Father has given you: "A new command I give you: Love one another. As I have loved you, so you must love one another" (John 13:34).

Your marriage destiny is to love your spouse.

TEST YOUR LOVE!

On a date in high school, I gauged my virility by gripping the handle of a vintage arcade game called the Love Tester. The feedback would be in the form of a light bulb glowing next to an adjective score. Top scores on the machine respectively were "UNCONTROLLABLE," "HOT STUFF," and "PASSIONATE." The lowest three were "HARMLESS," "CLAMMY," and "POOR FISH, TRY AGAIN," with the latter ranking swimming at the bottom of the pool.

If I got an embarrassing score, I would drop another quarter into the Love Tester slot and grip the metal handle again until I at least ranked a middle score of "WILD." I'm sure those games made millions off of vain young people like me.

Knowing that no one wants to be labeled a poor fish, Focus on the Family has commissioned a marriage assessment that will help you identify your relationship strengths *and* weaknesses based on the twelve topics in this book. (We guarantee it's more accurate than the Love Tester.) If you as a couple use this online tool, you'll have a better understanding of which areas in your marriage could use more attention. Plus you'll have access to other resources to help tune up your marriage.

Focus on the Family wants to ensure you are uncontrollably in love with your spouse. No clammy marriages allowed!

Visit www.CrazyLittleThingCalledMarriage.com to take the *free* assessment and receive a customized report.

THE LOOK OF LOVE

So, what does loving your spouse truly look like?

Let me illustrate the answer to this question. I recently was editing video curriculum that featured twenty of the best Christian marriage experts. They were offering advice for engaged couples.* We didn't script or tell the experts what to say, and we received some powerful biblical counsel.

As I watched all the experts—one right after the other—I was amazed at a particular theme that was repeated by the presenters: sacrifice. It's as if they all had read John 15:13 as their morning devotion: "Greater love has no one than this, that someone lay down his life for his friends" (ESV).

Sacrifice is what love looks like. It's giving up something you value (your time, money, comfort, or desires) for the sake of someone else whom you consider to have a greater value.[4]

It's relatively easy for me as an adult to serve someone—to help out or assist. I usually do that cheerfully. But it's a whole different story when serving someone costs me something.

I admit sacrificing for Erin can be a struggle. But I don't regret or resent it. In fact, the act of sacrificing now is one way I grow closer to God.

The culture says that sacrifice is a loss. In a biblical reckoning, sacrifice in marriage is a win-win situation.

That's what's so crazy about biblical marriage. There are twelve secrets—crazy countercultural secrets—that stem from Scriptures that, once embraced, will fill your marriage with intimacy, trust, and romance.

Let's look at "Romance Secret #1: True Love Commits."

---

* This amazing resource is the *Ready to Wed* DVD curriculum published by Focus on the Family/Tyndale, 2015.

TRUE LOVE COMMITS

There be three things which are too wonderful for me,
yea, four which I know not: The way of an eagle in the
air; the way of a serpent upon a rock; the way of a ship in
the midst of the sea; and the way of a man with a maid.
Proverbs 30:18-19, KJV

Hidden behind the 1990s matrimonial bling, as recorded in our wedding DVD, was a second life-changing concept.

There we stood, dressed in almost regal finery. She wore the customary white dress accented by a beaded headband with tulle exploding from the back. I wore a light-gray tux and a naively eager smile on my lips.

After vowing with solemnity and sincerity, the thought of till-death-do-us-part dedication was overtaken by the whirlwind celebrations. The toasts were made, the cake was cut, the garter tossed, and concern about commitment was cast aside with it.

The way I saw it back then, I'd found a girl and gotten married. I checked that off my life's to-do list and set my mind on other goals. Sure I knew I would have to buy an anniversary gift—diamonds are the fifth anniversary gift or are they the tenth?—and I figured I'd be in trouble with Erin if I didn't think of something romantic for Valentine's Day. But those two events were once a year with clearly defined parameters. Selfishly I knew that if I played my cards right and made Erin happy on those celebratory days, I'd probably be happy too, wink wink.

I'm ashamed to admit it, but I thought of marriage maintenance as something simple and routine, like setting the clocks an hour ahead or swapping out fresh batteries in the smoke detectors. The promise to cherish my wife was relegated to a couple of dates on the calendar.

I was soon going to reap the unhappy consequences of my ignorance and my cavalier approach to matrimonial commitment.

HURRICANE O

Fast-forward two weeks. Apparently Erin and I had spent more effort preparing for the perfect day instead of for the perfect relationship. While our wedding went off without a hitch, the "honeymoon was over" even before the honeymoon was over.

The setting? Hawaii. The problem? Definitely Erin. Or so I thought at the time. Here's how it happened . . .

> The "honeymoon was over" even before the honeymoon was over.

On the last day of our trip, we wanted to visit a tropical waterfall. You know the one on the travel agency posters: the white foaming water cutting through

gray granite towers and splashing into a pristine blue pool cir-
cumscribed by lush foliage bursting with the blooms of large,
red flowers. I'd mapped out a route, and we happily hiked to
the spot.

After arriving I stripped to my swim trunks and jumped
straight into the refreshing water, waiting for my lovely bride to
join me. This was going to be a swim to remember.

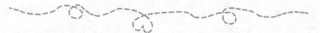

*It is just as crazy not to be crazy about Christ
as it is to be crazy about anything else.*

Peter Kreeft, *Jesus-Shock*

I motioned with outstretched arms and an irresistibly inviting look in my eyes.

But Erin stood on the bank, fully clothed, and, for some
inexplicable reason, *resisting*.

"Come on in," I beckoned.

She shook her head and simply pointed to a sign that read,
"NO SWIMMING."

The emotional weather changed as fast as a tropical storm.
Hurricane O moved in—O for Our First Big Fight.

The next few minutes were spent arguing, and after I finally
realized that she wasn't going to move, I shouted, "You just
ruined the honeymoon!"

Then I watched as she slipped into the jungle growth and
disappeared.

The majestic setting seemed to mock me. Externally my
world was perfect. Internally it was falling apart. (We'll hear

Erin's side of the story in "Romance Secret #4: True Love Fights for Peace." Stay tuned for how we learned the secret of not only reconciling arguments like this one, but also growing closer as a couple through the process.)

Somehow we smoothed over the spat during a luau, silently agreeing to avoid the topic. But over the next few months, waves of tension washed over us. The tide would pull them away before we could resolve them. We argued about in-laws, chores, and money. The stress of our jobs and my graduate school schedule seemed as if they would drown us.

I wondered, *What went wrong? Did I choose the wrong person?*

This marriage thing was supposed to be easy. After all, I was the son of Gary Smalley, relationship expert and marriage guru. Surely I knew how to reach out in love and recapture Erin's heart. But instead of coming up with ideas to calm the emotional storms, my efforts at communication blew things further out of control.

This man and this maid, who had been so in love, were now completely miserable.

A "Rocky" Start

Erin and I suffered from the devastation of Hurricane O and the following storms. Many days I felt as if our marriage foundation was washing away.

But it held fast.

Why? Because we'd had a "rocky" start.

And in the context of the Bible, that's a good thing!

Erin and I had one of the essential ingredients for a strong relationship. We'd built our marriage house on rock, as described in Jesus' parable. (See Matthew 7.) God's power held us together.

Before we became engaged, Erin and I had, as individuals, committed our lives to serving God and following His teachings in the Bible.

> *When I have learnt to love God better*
> *than my earthly dearest, I shall love my*
> *earthly dearest better than I do now.*
>
> C. S. Lewis, *Letters of C. S. Lewis*

I had been intentionally pursuing my faith since high school. When we got married, I was in seminary, burning the midnight oil studying systematic theology. Erin had made a commitment to intentional spiritual growth during college. As a couple, we were deciding whether to attend a Catholic or Evangelical church, but at least we knew that spiritual accord was essential. That commitment to God sustained us (and still does) during our stormy times.

Thy Treasure—Thy Heart

I love the word *wholehearted*. Erin and I have used it to title several of our marriage books. Wholehearted means "marked by complete earnest commitment."[1] Complete, earnest: these are the words I want defining my commitment to Erin.

A wholehearted commitment to marriage starts by recognizing its incredible value. Matthew 6:21 says, "For where your treasure is, there your heart will be also" (ESV). Commitment—fully and earnestly investing your whole heart—flows out of what you treasure. In other words, you will only invest in what you esteem. And the more committed you are to it, the more you'll invest.

Have you ever thought about what you like about your marriage or why Hebrews 13:4 says, "Marriage should be honored by all"? It's because you must regard your marriage with great respect.

Even though we had difficulties, Erin and I still valued some things. Here's the list as it was then:

- Having fun and laughing together
- Going on mission trips together
- Having someone to celebrate with
- Having sex
- Being with a best friend
- Being part of a team

What do you love about your marriage? Treasuring and honoring your marriage is vital, but it's not sufficient for a lifelong marriage. At some point a husband and wife need to decide to stay married for better, for worse, for richer, for poorer, in sickness and in health, till death do us part.

A WIDOW'S VOW

One scripture that's often quoted during marriage ceremonies reflects this commitment to God in a powerful way. It's from the Old Testament story of Ruth.

At first glance, the passage might not seem like strong marriage material; however, a Moabite widow's initial commitment to God and His people later defines one of the great love stories in the Bible. Ruth makes a simple, yet profound, vow to her mother-in-law, a displaced Israelite named Naomi. The formative foundation of that love rests on Ruth's pledge to follow the Lord. As we'll see, a commitment to honor God is the first step toward developing a marriage that can sustain lifelong passion.

The tension of Ruth's story develops upon the death of her husband, Mahlon, who provided financially for her and for Naomi while they lived in Moab. After Mahlon's death, Naomi decides to return to her homeland, Bethlehem. She forbids Ruth from coming with her and encourages her to find a new husband from among the Moabites. The story picks up in Ruth 1:16 (ESV):

> *A commitment to honor God is the first step toward developing a marriage that can sustain lifelong passion.*

Ruth said [to Naomi], "Do not urge me to leave you or to return from following you. For where you go I will go, and where you lodge I will lodge. Your people shall be my people, and your God my God."

Ruth makes this promise, in essence, pledging her life to serve the living God.

SNUFF OUT YOUR CANDLE

Ruth clearly takes the first step in preparing for marriage by committing her life to the God of the Israelites. Next, she vows to leave her life with the Moabites behind. She denounces her former polytheistic religion, her homeland, and her emotional and financial ties to blood kin. Ruth never once looks back, vowing to serve God and Naomi until she dies.

> Where you die I will die, and there will I be buried. May the LORD do so to me and more also if anything but death parts me from you. (v. 17, ESV)

Ruth shows her commitment to God and His people is unto death—as is the marriage covenant.

But there are two kinds of death. One takes place before physical death: dying to self. There are only two passages in the Bible that tell us to do something "daily." One is to "encourage one another daily" (Hebrews 3:13); the other is "take up [your] cross daily" (Luke 9:23). Taking up our crosses refers to how Christ made the ultimate sacrifice—His life. Likewise I am to lay down my life—my selfish desires—and sacrificially serve my wife.

We knew we were loved, we knew the Lord was head of our house, we knew where the lines were drawn, we were safe.

Elisabeth Elliot, *Love Has a Price Tag*

"Dying to self" daily is a key to not only the Christian life but also to lifelong love and romance with your spouse. Part of that "death" means leaving your past life as a single adult and creating a new culture based on the union of one man and one woman. A second essential aspect of marital success is that individuals must leave their past life behind and commit to a future with their spouse.

On our wedding day, Erin and I likewise vowed to leave our single lives behind and form a new bond, one life as couple. We chose to symbolize this aspect of marriage by using a unity candle at our wedding.

FLAMING LOVE

The unity candle tradition works like this: At the beginning of the wedding, two lit candles sit on the altar; the candles represent the lives of the couple before marriage. Holding long candle lighters with a bell-shaped cone at the end, the man and woman each touch the wicks of the candle lighters to the flame of the first candle. Next they snuff out the first candles with the cones. Finally, in unison, they light a third candle, which symbolizes their unity.

Did you notice something powerful in that short ceremony? It's the "dying to self" symbolism. The original two candles—representing separate lives—are snuffed in order to show a commitment to the one new life the couple is beginning together.

TRICK CANDLES

Unfortunately, the circumstances surrounding my married life didn't parallel the unity tradition. In my soul I had one of those trick candles that relights, because the desires of my former life kept right on smoldering.

I knew that I should "leave" my old life and "cleave" only to my wife as the King James version of Genesis commands a man to do. But under pressure in the first months of our marriage, I was double-minded. Memories of my independent, Greg-only priorities would warm my thoughts causing me to want to re-kindle my single (translated: self-centered) way of life.

I wanted to spend money on CDs and Erin wanted to pay bills. I wanted to play basketball five days a week or watch televi-sion till the wee hours of the morning. Erin had other plans for me, such as washing dishes. I thought living as a caveman was fine; I had no desire to buy into her Martha Stewart standards.

As I struggled with the difficult realities of marriage, I let discontent weigh down my soul.

Erin struggled in the quicksand even more than I did. De-pression and anxiety threatened to suffocate her. At that time in my life, immaturity and pride kept me from taking respon-sibility for our problems, and so Erin sought counseling alone.

We were stuck, anchored at the island of self-pity, each of us surreptitiously longing for the shores of singlehood.

LESSONS FROM *THE ART OF WAR*

Ironically, concepts revealed in the ancient book *The Art of War* helped us make peace. I finally realized that marriage is a lifelong battle against selfishness, a strong adversary capable of giving our love mortal wounds. I had yet to commit myself fully to the fight for our marriage.

I found inspirational principles for that fight in an unusual source.

Notes from a Chinese General

If you're in a battle, you need to seek counsel. The words are from Chinese philosopher-general Sun Tzu directing those who want to protect and advance their countries in the essential art of war. He noted in the sixth century BC:

> [War] is a matter of life and death, a road either to safety or to ruin. Hence it is a subject of inquiry which can on no account be neglected.[2]

If you replace the word *war* with *marriage*, the message is profound for couples, perhaps even more so than for generals. I wanted a successful marriage. No, that's not exactly right. I wanted a fun, adventurous, passionate, all-consuming desire for Erin to dominate my thoughts and define my priorities. And I wanted her to feel the same way about me and our marriage. But we were nowhere close to winning the battle because we were neglecting something that threatened the life of our marriage. We were headed toward ruin, not safety. We needed to learn an important lesson about waging the war against self-centeredness.

Ditch the Idea of Divorce

In those early days, the D-word was unspoken, but the menace of it permeated our arguments. Our verbal battles would escalate to the point where I'd try to put words into Erin's mouth, such as "Are you saying I should leave?" or "Why would you want to stay with me?" Neither of us wanted separation, but our inability to resolve our fights played out in melodrama. The one-liners were lead anchors of dissatisfaction, cleverly packed away in our emotional baggage. Until we threw the idea of divorce overboard, we couldn't sail away from our problems.

Mentioning divorce showed that we weren't taking God's

warning in Matthew 19:6 seriously: "No one should separate what God has joined together" (NIrv).

When divorce isn't an option, commitment forces a couple to work through problems. The idea of living out my marriage in misery frightened me. I could choose to either run away or work to resolve the problems. Because I was committed to God and His values (see Malachi 2:16), I gave up the option of divorce. I had only one course of action: I chose to fight for Erin's love even if it killed me.

> *When divorce isn't an option, commitment forces a couple to work through problems.*

Burn the Boats

The idea to sabotage a retreat option and stick to the war no matter the cost is another concept described in *The Art of War*:*

> Burn your baggage and impedimenta, throw away your stores and provisions, choke up the wells, destroy your cooking-stoves, and make it plain to your men that they cannot survive, but must fight to the death.[3]

> When your army has crossed the border, you should burn the boats and bridges, in order to make it clear to everybody that you have no hankering after home.[4]

In any battle, the option of retreat or "hankering after home" must be eliminated. But even more drastic than burning a land

---

*If you recently read this story in *Ready to Wed* (Tyndale/Focus on the Family, 2015), I apologize for the repetition, but it's the best example I know to convey this important concept.

bridge is destroying your means to cross an ocean. I call this the "burn the boats" marriage mentality. It's the ultimate show of commitment.

You may be wondering which commanders acted upon this extreme advice. Legends say that a Berber named Taric the One-Eyed burned his army's boats after landing along the coast of Spain in 711.[5] The tactic was described in the Roman myth of Aeneas when the goddess Juno tried to keep the Trojans in Sicily.[6] Another legend tells of Alexander the Great burning his ships after landing to conquer Persia circa 334 BC.[7] But by far my favorite "burn the boats" story features the politically incorrect Hernán Cortés. (His ideals were atrocious, but his methods were courageous.)

Imagine you're a Spanish soldier, arriving on a mysterious foreign coast and facing the Aztec warriors, ferocious men wearing wood helmets and dressed as jaguars.[8] The leader of the Aztecs, Montezuma II, has rebuffed countless armies. And then Cortés orders you to light the ships' sails on fire! As the fire blazes bright and hot, you realize you must fight to the death. There's no turning back. Your survival is now dependent on your ability to defeat the Aztecs.[9]

Likewise, if spouses perceive that conquering marriage issues is the only option, their choices are focused on improving the odds of marriage survival. Spouses choose wisely when they know that their life destinies are fused to another person's well-being. They talk about their feelings, even if it's painful, instead of pretending "everything is fine." They refuse to dwell on the negatives when their spouse ruffles their emotional feathers. They let "love and faithfulness never leave" them (Proverbs 3:3), even if their spouse has an illness or life-changing accident. "Burning the boats" means a spouse has promised to stick out the battle, not just today but forever.

After we caught on to the "burn the boats" way of thinking, divorce wasn't an option for Erin and me. We never even joke about it or allude to leaving.

COMMITMENT ROMANCE SECRET

So, Greg, you're probably asking, *what's the secret to better romance you promised if I commit unconditionally to my marriage?*

Research shows a marriage commitment yields a more satisfying relationship on all levels.[10] Guys, women respond when they know you'll "die to self" for them. Trust and security shore up a woman's heart, and she'll be more likely to bond emotionally.[11]

> *Research shows a marriage commitment yields a more satisfying relationship on all levels.*

Ladies, men hesitate to invest unless they know there's a payoff. Let your husband know you'll support him and your marriage no matter what. One researcher concluded that "a man tends to give most completely to a woman once he has decided, *She is my future.*"[12]

Our Future

In 1992, Jason Heinrich was diagnosed with a rare form of cancer. Fear and pain entered his six-year-old perspective.

The malignant cells destroyed his right femur, and the bone was removed. When he was twelve, a surgeon offered a choice: adjust to life with crutches, or try an experimental orthopedic procedure that had, so far, never been done in the United States. The new implant was cutting-edge and would fit the needs of a young person like Jason.

The cure was extensive—spanning more than seven years. The treatments were excruciating—his leg was maimed by an accidental instrument failure. The ordeal was exhausting—the emotional and physical toll on Jason's mind and body left him old beyond his years.

But by high school, Jason had allowed God to replace his fear and dread of hospitals with a compelling goal: to become a perfusionist to help other people with life-threatening conditions. Today, with a degree in biochemistry and a job as a patient care technician, he's anticipating an interview to enter a Perfusion Technology Master's program in the Midwest.

Likewise, Erin and I wanted God to replace our relationship pain with something positive. That's why we decided to commit to marriage ministry as a couple, to redeem our relationship—to fight the cancer of selfishness—in order to help others. We set sail on a new adventure together, and we've never once looked back.

If you would like ideas for date nights based on the theme of this chapter, visit *crazylittlethingcalledmarriage.com*. You'll also find thought-provoking questions for couples and small groups.

In "Romance Secret #2," you'll discover that commitment is also the key to spiritual intimacy.

TRUE LOVE SEEKS GOD

Be completely humble and gentle; be patient,
bearing with one another in love.
Make every effort to keep the unity of the
Spirit through the bond of peace.

Ephesians 4:2-3

If Sun Tzu were writing *The Art of War* today, twenty-seven centuries later, he'd have to address the realities of nuclear technology and the arms race. He'd have to develop an anti-missile plan ("If [the enemy] is secure at all points, be prepared for him"[1]) and figure out how to effectively use remotely piloted aircraft. ("Appear where you are not expected")[2] To be competitive, General Tzu would also need the atomic bomb. And for the A-bomb, he'd need plutonium.

I did a little research on that radioactive element, and I was intrigued. Not only by the history of the Manhattan Project and how difficult plutonium is to transport, but also by how many aspects of martial intimacy parallel the quest for plutonium.

Love is not just looking at each other,
it's looking in the same direction.
Antoine de Saint-Exupéry, novelist

Yes, I know that sounds crazy and more than a little odd: how could having a substance with the chemical potential to destroy the planet be like communion with the Creator? While there are some obvious differences, let me explain the surprising similarities between a spiritual marriage and PU-239, the form of plutonium used to fuel nuclear power:

- Both are highly desired and yet difficult to procure.
- Both have transformative powers.
- If you mix the chemicals in the wrong order, you get the wrong substance.
- Once the source is discovered, the finders have incredible power over their enemies.

And wait, there's extra credit! Did you know that any form of plutonium is rarely found in nature? Scientists must deliberately create it in a lab. Likewise, spiritual intimacy in marriage seldom occurs without effort. It must be intentionally developed.

For couples who work with each other to produce a faith-based power (think plutonium) for their marriages, the effort is worth it. Here's a sampling of some studies which demonstrate that couples who are spiritually close are happier or better adjusted than their nonspiritual counterparts:

- Couples who attend church together and have similar religious views are happier, live longer, and are less likely to engage in problem drinking.[3]
- Spiritually intimate couples who are raising their first child experience more positive interaction during the child's first year.[4]
- Older couples who develop compassionate love based on marriage as a sacred commitment have high relationship quality.[5]

SPIRITUAL ARCHITECTURE 101

Developing spiritual intimacy in marriage builds on the principles revealed in "Romance Secret #1: True Love Commits." We've found that a commitment to God as individuals is the precursor for couples who want a deep faith connection. The Bible hero Ruth made a radical commitment to the people of the living God before she entered a marriage covenant. Erin and I remained steadfast during our tumultuous times because we each had first dedicated our single selves to seeking God and His ways; we began our "rocky" relationship by building on the foundation of biblical truth. Then we learned how to "burn the boats" and to look forward rather than back at our single lives. In the Smalley house, we chose early on to follow the Lord despite what the opposing cultural messages told us.

> God, who gives "immeasurably more than all we ask or imagine," honors couples who seek to grow together spiritually.

The second secret to a romantic relationship requires taking another faith step: together the couple needs to seek God.

Scripture encourages spouses to focus on Christ not only in their individual lives but also in their marriage. And God, who gives "immeasurably more than all we ask or imagine," honors couples who seek to grow together spiritually (Ephesians 3:20).

Throughout the Bible, the inspired authors used the metaphor of constructing a building to illustrate faith development. We've already seen the house-built-on-rock parable in Matthew 7. The apostle Paul offered the believers in Ephesus a familiar example of a building project to teach the church. I believe this passage gives an insightful explanation of how spiritual intimacy works:

> You are . . . members of God's household, built on the foundation of the apostles and prophets, with Christ Jesus himself as the chief cornerstone. In him the whole building is joined together and rises to become a holy temple in the Lord. And in him you too are being built together to become a dwelling in which God lives by his Spirit. (Ephesians 2:19-22)

These verses show that God, the Master Architect, builds the community of believers. The concrete metaphor of a building gives us a glimpse into how the mysterious and immaterial Spirit lives among believers in Jesus Christ.

God forms the community of believers into a household, a home for His Spirit.

Think Like an Ephesian

Notice that the building is called a *household*, a *temple*, and a *dwelling*. For the Christian, life and worship can't be separated. All of life for the citizens of God's community is an act of worship. Consequently, this home functions also as a temple.

The early Ephesians were not Jewish or culturally linked to the history of Solomon's Temple. Neither were they geographically close to Jerusalem, where the second Jewish holy temple stood.[6] But they nevertheless understood the concept of a temple, albeit a pagan one. Since elaborate temples to the Greek gods stood near the center of the city marketplace and took years to build, the Ephesian citizens most likely had witnessed the construction of one temple or another. They would have seen the builders place the cornerstone, the starting point of the foundation. The words "rises to become a holy temple" probably would have evoked the image of the Temple of Artemis, a beautiful, twenty-seven columned marble structure, which is listed among the seven wonders of the ancient world.[7] (See Acts 19:23-34.) The Ephesians' temple concept was pagan in practice, but the intent of Paul's meaning was clear even to that non-Jewish community: God's temple is not made of cold, hard marble but of living, breathing men and women dedicated to Him.

> God's temple is not made of cold, hard marble but of living, breathing men and women dedicated to Him.

Temple Transformation

Think of Christian marriage as a micro-community or a mini-church—it's a temple built for two. A Christian marriage—*your marriage*—becomes a temple where God's Spirit lives if you commit your ways to biblical principles. You can't help but have a dynamic spiritual relationship when the Creator of love is in your midst.

Marriage, a wholehearted union, is made even more intimate when the husband and wife become "one flesh" (Mark 10:8). So in one sense spiritual marriage math is this: 1 + 1 = 1. But here's another way to calculate it: 1 + 1 = 3, because when a man and a woman are bonded in the spiritual realm, God joins them and adds His powerful presence to their union. He creates an incredible synergy between the husband and wife.

> *A married person does not live in isolation.*
> *He or she has made a promise, a pledge, a*
> *vow, to another person. Until that vow is*
> *fulfilled and the promise is kept, the individual*
> *is in debt to his marriage partner.*
>
> R. C. Sproul, theologian, author and pastor

Remember the PU-239 we talked about earlier? That powerful substance is made from another element, uranium, specifically two varieties named U-235 and U-238. The process called nuclear fission results from a chemical shell-swapping sleight of hand with slow-moving neutrons. The resulting power is a single fission event that can yield over two-hundred-million times the energy of the neutron that triggered it![8]

When a man and a woman form their temple in Christian marriage, a *new* element or entity is formed. A couple with God in their midst has more potential power than the normal "chemistry" described in romantic relationships. It's the power of the Holy Spirit.

To some of you, all this talk about "spiritual intimacy" seems pie in the sky, ethereal, esoteric, and elusive. You believe it would be more realistic to find that PU-239 in the hardware aisle at Walmart. You may doubt whether you can achieve this type of spiritual union. But I assure you, learning how to connect with your spouse spiritually via mind, soul, body, and strength is a heavenly gift that manifests in down-to-earth marriages.

Beginning in this chapter and in each subsequent chapter, I'm going to show you how to capture spiritual intimacy in a rubber-meets-the-road relationship—how to align your marriage with biblical priorities so it's strong and passion-filled. But to lay the foundation, I first must tell you how Erin and I messed up (yes, *again*), and then how we allowed God to fix it.

Spiritual Sequoias

I brought some unhealthy mental constructs into our marriage mix because I had a skewed opinion of what it means to be a spiritual leader. My family background includes growing up surrounded by "spiritual sequoias"—that's how I've come to think of people who are strong leaders and mature in Christ.

Giant sequoias live thousands of years and can push their trunks as high as twenty-five stories, seemingly reaching heaven. Their unusual size and grandeur attracts attention, bringing in tourists by the millions every year.[9] The massive trees have a lot in common with Christian leaders like my father, who seem larger than life. Like giant sequoias, "spiritual giants" are strong and amazingly suited to thrive even in hostile climates.

Surrounded by Giants

I grew up with my parents' friends stopping by the house or meeting us at restaurants or other venues. By the time I was eleven, my dad's first book was on track to sell more than a million copies.[10] His career as a speaker was taking off as well, and he traveled all over the country to lecture on marriage. Famous Christian notables such as John Trent, Corrie ten Boom, Michael W. Smith, Billy and Ruth Graham, Kay Arthur, Chuck Norris, Josh McDowell (my mom actually dated him before she dated my dad), James and Shirley Dobson, Chuck Swindoll, and Keith Green trekked in and out of my life, leaving their impressions on my mind and heart.

"You can be more effective together than apart. In a truly healthy relationship, we enable each other to accomplish more than we could have done alone. This was His plan."

Francis Chan, *You and Me Forever*

Then I went to grad school where some amazing teachers invested in me. Dr. Gary Oliver was one. He's not only a respected scholar and author but also a man of grace and compassion. Students on campus flocked to him for counseling, encouragement, and prayer.

Erin and I had been invited to his home on several occasions, and one room in particular will forever be seared into my memory. He and his late wife had part of their living room set aside for their morning devotion times. The Olivers would rise early and—still wearing their bathrobes—sit in two cozy chairs, cups of hot coffee at the ready. There they would meet the Lord together, every day, with Scripture reading and prayer.

In the shadows

I could have looked heavenward and seen the light source that blessed these giants; instead, I looked at my life and felt inadequate. I let the long shadows of their great presence darken the perception I had of my spiritual gifts. There didn't seem to be a way I could measure up to these faith-filled sequoias.

I wasn't the only one who noticed I was immature. My wife also found me falling short of her standards, asking me when we were going to pray and being shocked that I wasn't more like my father in leadership areas. Before I figured out the secret to connecting spiritually with Erin, I was root bound for a couple of years, cultivating only the misconception that I was a poor leader and therefore a spiritual failure.

WHY I DUCKED MY SPIRITUAL DYNASTY

The mistake I made in the early years of marriage was trying to avoid failure because I wasn't a strong spiritual leader. I hated feeling as if I couldn't measure up to my dad or Gary Oliver. At the time, I would avoid failure—ignore it, downplay it, or pretend the whole scenario didn't exist. I dropped the leadership scepter but not on purpose; when failure surrounded me,

I slunk away. I became paralyzed and immobile. I numbed out to the point that I became inactive. I withdrew from spiritual leadership by avoiding praying or going to church with Erin.

As a marriage counselor, I now know that, like me, many introverted or insecure or uninformed husbands initially struggle with leading spiritually in the home. Some of the reasons are because they . . .

- have misconceptions about what it means to be a spiritual leader;
- never had a good spiritual leader as a role model;
- believe that their relationship with God is great and they don't need to work at connecting with God;
- lack confidence either in their Bible knowledge or skills as a leader;
- feel intimidated by their wife's intense relationship with God;
- shy away from power-struggles with a strong-willed or a dominant wife or think their wife won't submit to their leadership;
- have more introverted or passive personalities than their wife and that makes leadership more difficult;
- prefer a more light-hearted approach to spirituality that can clash with their wife's more somber style;
- are more comfortable being spontaneous rather than structured.

As a result of factors such as these, many a man will abdicate his spiritual headship, his place on the "throne" as spiritual head of the house.

If a husband walks away from his throne, one of two things may happen. First is that the seat will remain empty, and the influence of God's Spirit will be lost and slowly fade like those neon glow sticks sold at amusement parks.

The second scenario is that his wife will take ownership of the chair. She'll reupholster it or drape a tapestry across the back. There she'll drink her tea or coffee, leaving the cups on a nearby table; her books and craft baskets will stack up on the floor. The longer she sits there, the more the foam cushions will conform to her feminine frame. The scents from her shampoo and perfume will saturate the fabric. It will look, feel, and smell like her chair. *Eventually, no one will remember the throne was ever his.*

To many couples, letting the wife take the lead of the spiritual leadership at home can feel good at first, especially if the wife is a go-getter and the man is more passive or introverted. The question then is this: If she's got the desire and the ability, what's wrong with her taking charge?

Typically shame and resentment, not peace, result from swapping the spiritual roles of a man and wife.

The short answer goes back to the PU-239 analogy: if you mix chemicals in the wrong order, you get unintended results, often hazardous ones. Typically shame and resentment, not peace, result from swapping the spiritual roles of a man and wife.

To illustrate, I'll have to tell you what happened to me and Erin. The timeframe is now two years into our marriage. We had a daughter, Taylor, who brought love and challenges in nearly equal amounts into our lives. I was pretty much my same lackadaisical self, not interested in my spiritual leadership role. But Erin, an exhausted nurse and new mother, sat on my abandoned throne, scepter in hand.

God's Order for Your Marriage Dynasty

I'm the first to broadcast that Erin is an amazing, intelligent woman and wife, a practically perfect modern Proverbs 31 example. (Any day now I'm expecting her to present me with a red robe she wove by hand out of flax fibers.)

I'm still discovering the layers of gifts and talents that God has given to her. I encourage her to follow her desires to minister at church or through her work. I lean on her to organize the household duties and care for the castle while I'm away speaking. But she can't do her role well if I don't support her in the home the way God intended.

> *As God by creation made two of one, so again by marriage He made one of two.*
> Thomas Adams, 17th century pastor and author

Early on she initiated the spiritual disciplines of prayer, service, and study. "We need to pray for so-and-so and such-and-such," she'd say. I now understand that one of Erin's spiritual gifts is intercessory prayer. This used to intimidate me. When she thought about praying for someone, I used to think, *What is wrong with me? I should have thought to pray for that person.* I took her reminders to pray—no matter how gentle and encouraging—as signals that I was failure.

On Sundays I was so tired she had to coax me to church. Every so often she'd sign us up for duties I had little interest in. Once I found myself in a Sunday school class helping with the wee ones. I zoned out while Erin taught the lesson. My mind would wander to important questions like why kids always peeled off the wrappers of the Crayolas or how I was going to get Goldfish dust out of my pants pockets.

She'd attend Bible meetings with other women and want to talk about the scripture truths she was studying. Instead of being excited about her learning and wanting to share in it, I turned away. I already was flooded with theology at seminary during the day, and I didn't want my evenings waterlogged with more.

Illumination

Remember I told you my dad is a great leader and counselor? He is that giant spiritual sequoia. One day after he and I had taught together at a marriage seminar in Clovis, New Mexico, he pushed me out of the shadow of his legacy so that my gifts— not his—were illuminated.

We sat in a Thai restaurant, just talking and relaxing. My dad started the conversation by explaining what the Lord had taught him about leadership during one of his morning prayer-run meetings with God.

Knowing that my dad ran and prayed simultaneously for hours every week set off my insecurities. I could run the distance, but I could only focus on prayer for maybe thirty-five seconds. I felt outclassed.

"Yeah, you're the great leader," I said, launching my sarcastic missile. "Even my wife wonders why I'm not more like you."

My dad said, "Greg, I see an amazing spiritual leader in you."

I had no idea what he was talking about. *Me, a leader? I'm the guy with a miserable marriage and who can barely remember John 3:16.*

"A man can give spiritual leadership in all kinds of ways," he said. "It's more than reading the Bible and memorizing scripture." He looked deep into my eyes and spoke these words of encouragement:

I see a man who loves his wife and daughter wholeheartedly.

I see a man who serves his wife and daughter sacrificially.

I see a man who provides financially for his family.

I see a man who takes his wife and daughter to church.

I see a man who protects his family.

I see a man who resolves conflict biblically.

I see a man who is involved in the parenting of his daughter. He provides discipline and emotional support, watches *Veggie Tales* with her, reads Bible stories to her, plays with her, and shows her how to respect her parents and God.

I see a man who takes responsibility and seeks forgiveness when he makes a mistake.

I see a man who prays with his wife and for his daughter.

Never again have I beat myself up for not waking at dawn and leading Erin in a study of 1 Chronicles. God used my dad that day to give me a renewed spiritual vision for what spiritual leadership really means.

Men, Lead Like Jesus

I want to challenge men to let go of preconceived notions about what it means to be a spiritual leader—where they're only focused on spiritual disciplines. I want to challenge each woman to broaden her definition of what it means to be a spiritual leader and to notice all the ways that her husband loves and cares for his family.

Finding a place of spiritual intimacy with your spouse should feel comfortable and practical, like a pair of broken-in hiking boots. Seeking God's plan for your marriage takes intentionality, but it

It might be an uphill climb, but the view at the top is fantastic.

doesn't leave blisters. It might be an uphill climb, but the view at the top is fantastic.

God has gifted every person with specific strengths. Certain gifts help men lead the family toward God, using His methods of humility and grace.

A man can give spiritual leadership in all kinds of ways. I've listed several below that I've found in Scripture. We've already looked at the principles behind the first few and a several more on the list will be discussed in depth later in this book.

A spiritual man . . .

- leaves his parents and cleaves to his wife—1 + 1 = 1 (Genesis 2:24, Ephesians 5:31);
- is faithful (Malachi 2:15);
- serves sacrificially (Ephesians 5:25);
- loves his wife (Colossians 3:19);
- becomes involved in the parenting of his children (Proverbs 22:6);
- provides financially for his family (1 Timothy 5:8);
- cherishes and nourishes his wife (Ephesians 5:28);
- resolves conflict biblically, keeping temper in check (Ephesians 4:31-32);
- asks for forgiveness and forgives others (Matthew 5:23-24);

- honors his wife (1 Peter 3:7);
- teaches and models a proper respect for authority (Romans 13:1);
- and provides an encouraging environment (Hebrews 3:13).

Men, having the authority to lead your wife in the ways of God is not a ticket to go on a power trip; you're called to the highest level of self-sacrifice there is, with Jesus as your role model (Ephesians 5:25). FYI, that's the humble Jesus who didn't "consider equality with God something to be grasped," (Philippians 2:6) and the obedient Jesus who "died for sins once for all, the righteous for the unrighteous, to bring [us] to God" (1 Peter 3:18).

Robertson McQuilkin

In whatever manner a man leads his family—if he's being led by God's Spirit and subduing his selfish desires—humility and sacrificial love will be the overall signature style. One man who embodied this style was the late Robertson McQuilkin.

I heard his story years ago, and I've never forgotten it. So deep was Robertson McQuilkin's sacrificial love for his wife, Muriel, that he gave up a prestigious job to care for her after early onset Alzheimer's destroyed her ability to be left alone. Devastated, McQuilkin watched his life partner transition from being a dynamic personality into a faded shadow of herself.[11]

The letter McQuilkin wrote to Columbia University upon his resignation as president brings me almost to tears:

> My dear wife, Muriel, has been in failing mental health
> for about 12 years. So far I have been able to carry both
> her ever-growing needs and my leadership responsibility

at Columbia. But recently it has become apparent that Muriel is contented most of the time she is with me and almost none of the time I am away from her. It is not just "discontent." She is filled with fear—even terror—that she has lost me and always goes in search of me when I leave home. So it is clear to me that she needs me now, full-time. . . .

The decision was made, in a way, 42 years ago when I promised to care for Muriel "in sickness and in health . . . till death do us part." . . . Integrity has something to do with it. But so does fairness. She has cared for me fully and sacrificially all these years; if I cared for her for the next 40 years I would not be out of her debt. Duty, however, can be grim and stoic. But there is more: I love Muriel. She is a delight to me—her childlike dependence and confidence in me, her warm love, occasional flashes of that wit I used to relish so, her happy spirit and tough resilience in the face of her continual distressing frustration. I don't *have* to care for her. I *get* to! It is a high honor to care for so wonderful a person.[12]

A Wife Like Priscilla

Wives, you're called to help your husband with his leadership tasks, each deferring to the other, but ultimately respecting and enhancing his leadership (Ephesians 5:33). Priscilla, wife of Aquila, was faithful, and the New Testament always mentions her in the same sentence as her husband—they were exiled together, were converted together, and worked side-by-side.[13]

You can also find that kind of marital closeness. Here are some tips on developing that spiritual intimacy you crave. First, if you've taken over as head of the house, move out of that role so it becomes your husband's again. Next, go through this short inventory and see what you can do this week:

- Help your husband discover the truth about his leadership gifts by identifying his strengths. Go over the list in the previous section, mark the ones your husband does well, and then add your own.
- Identify your spiritual gifts so that he knows how to support you in your God-given role.

ERIN'S INSIGHTS ON LEADERSHIP

When Greg and I were first married, I unintentionally had enormously high expectations of him as the spiritual leader in our home. I wanted a man with the moral conviction of missionary Olympian Eric Liddell, the charisma of evangelist Billy Graham, and the courage of pastor-rebel Dietrich Bonhoeffer—all that combined with the gentleness of Mr. Rogers. If I couldn't find that, I wanted something attainable, something I'd seen and admired in a real person. Without even realizing it, that something was a younger version of Greg's dad, Gary Smalley, who in my mind was a spiritual giant.

I came from a family where my mom was the main spiritual influence for my brother and me. This dynamic created the perfect formula for spiritual relationship disaster. As it turned out, early in our marriage Greg did not act much like Gary, who dedicated hours to prayer and Scripture memorization. So I jumped in and took over—much like my mom had. I continually requested that Greg would pray or talk about the Bible. I signed us up for small groups and church activities without asking, because I thought it would encourage Greg to engage. I unintentionally went on making choices because I was very aware that he was withdrawn and wasn't a willing participant in spiritual things.

- Embrace the good ways that you and your husband work well together right now.
- Encourage him daily.

Cultivating a Thriving Shared Spiritual Relationship

The last book of the Old Testament, Malachi, tells about the people of Judah during a time when they thought that God had

---

I now see that I gave Greg very little time to grow and develop as the spiritual leader. He had never been in this role—but I still somehow expected him to have the maturity of his sixty-year-old father! Basically, I wanted him to lead devotionals the way I had watched his dad do every morning, to know instinctively when I needed to pray with him, and to be the one seeking church involvement with vim and vigor.

Greg didn't yet have that spiritual wisdom developed over years of experience, and his style of relating to God was also different from my father-in-law's. For example, Greg is an introvert, with a super laid-back personality. He connects with God by being outdoors. But early on, when things didn't happen the way I thought they would, I jumped into super-sonic spiritual mode and essentially took over. Greg reacted to my flurry of activity by feeling like a failure as the spiritual head in our home. Worse, he ended up withdrawing from me spiritually.

Looking back twenty-four years, if I had to do it all over again, I'd offer more grace and initiate more discussion about my hopes and expectations. I would notice and praise the good things that Greg did, those things that were beyond prayer and Bible study. I now see that a spiritual marriage relationship grows with time, just like every other part of a marriage relationship.

forgotten them. The prophet Malachi responded to them, in essence, that the people were the ones who had forgotten God and His ways. Malachi 2:14 specifically points out the Israelites had broken faith in their marriage covenants. The next verse says: "God, not you, made marriage. His Spirit inhabits even the smallest details of marriage . . . so guard the spirit of marriage within you" (Malachi 2:15, MSG).

By guarding that spirit, you are honoring God, who will, in turn, honor you. Here are three ways to "guard" the spirit (your spiritual relationship) of marriage within you.

1. Identify your spiritual relationship roadblocks.

Do any of these factors affect your marriage and the level of closeness you feel toward your spouse? Check the three that are most likely to derail your relationship, and make a plan to improve in that area this week.

- busyness
- differing spiritual levels
- sin
- differing way of expressing spiritual love
- lack of interest
- conflict
- closed or hardened hearts
- resentment or lack of forgiveness

At the Smalley home, busyness sometimes overwhelms us. We've learned to relax and not be so rigid in thinking that we *must* be in church every Sunday. Every once in a while, the family is exhausted, and I hook up the computer to the TV. The whole family watches the service online. We sing at the top of our lungs and even dance to the music. We laugh and then talk about what each person learned. We have some of the best conversations about God while together as a family.

2. Incorporate daily spiritual disciplines into your relationship.

Figure out ways to add more intentional spiritual activities in your marriage. Make sure they match your style and passions.

- Pray (praying for and with each other)
- Study the Bible
- Worship corporately (church)
- Give to a special cause, and unite in sacrifice to do it (tithe 10 percent).
- Witness
- Download sermons and listen to them.
- Choose a day to fast together.
- Listen to praise and worship music.
- Observe the Sabbath as a day of rest.

3. Take Advantage of Everyday Spiritual Moments

Be aware of opportunities that you can work into your day-to-day routines so you can increase your spiritual connection times during the day. This concept is based on the Old Testament principle, "Teach [God's ways] to your children, talking about them when you sit at home and when you walk along the road, when you lie down and when you get up" (Deuteronomy 11:19).

- Pray for your spouse before you leave the house to "encourage one another daily." (Hebrews 3:13)
- Driving together can be a time to reflect on this question: What is one thing that God is teaching you?

- Listen to praise and worship music together.
- Pray together before bed.
- At the dinner table have access to Bible verses to read aloud or pray for people outside your immediate family.
- Text an uplifting blessing for your partner or an inspirational Bible verse.

Here's what Erin and I are working on this month. We sometimes struggle to be disciplined in one of our favorite times together as a couple—praying together before falling asleep. If I get to bed before Erin, I begin checking email or reading the news on my cell phone. Then Erin comes to bed and sees me with my phone. That's a cue to her that she's forgotten to email someone about something. So she takes out her phone. Then I see that she's busy, so I move on to the next story or email. The cycle goes on and the minutes fritter away. Occasionally we let our busyness steal precious minutes of prayer time because by the time we start, our heads are full of administrative tasks, depressing news, or the latest Pinterest post. We're aware of this bad habit and are striving to curtail the technology use before prayer time.

NUCLEAR POWER FOR COUPLES

Like nuclear fission, couples with God as their cornerstone have more potential power than they could ever imagine. One of the key concepts in this chapter is learning to tap into that power through intentionally connecting to God and to each other. I've touched on a portion of Ephesians 3:20 in the section Spiritual Architecture 101. Here is that verse again with more context:

I pray that you, being rooted and established in love, may have power, together with all the saints, to grasp how wide and long and high and deep is the love of Christ, and to know this love that surpasses knowledge— that you may be filled to the measure of all the fullness of God. (Ephesians 3:17-19)

The key to God's unlimited power source is to practice daily spiritual disciplines together—that's the "being rooted and established in love" part of the passage. Remember that you don't have to be one of those couples who rise in the morning together and devote an hour to prayer. The goal is to work toward finding additional ways you and your spouse can connect spiritually within the scope of the husband's leadership style as he supports and nurtures his wife's spiritual gifting. Here are some of Erin's and my favorite spiritual disciplines for couples:

- Praying together (Matthew 18:19)
- Using encouraging words with each other (Hebrews 3:13)
- Studying God's Word together (2 Timothy 3:16-17)
- Attending church together (Hebrews 10:25)
- Giving and uniting in sacrifice to do it (2 Corinthians 9:6-8)
- Witnessing and making disciples (Matthew 28:18-20)
- Caring for orphans and widows (James 1:27)
- Studying sermons together (Acts 2:42)
- Meditating on Scripture (Joshua 1:8)
- Fasting together (Matthew 6:16-18)
- Memorizing Scripture (Psalm 119:11)

- Participating in praise and worship (Psalm 95:1-2)
- Observing a day of rest (Exodus 20:8-11)
- Reading a devotional together (Psalm 119:105)
- Participating in Sunday school or small groups
  (1 Thessalonians 5:11)
- Keeping a journal of the specific ways God has helped
  our marriage (1 Samuel 7:12)

As we plug into the right power source, we have what we need to live out the second part of the great commandment: "Love your neighbor as yourself" (Mark 12:31). This gives us an important order. First, we love God wholeheartedly, and then we love others. The point is that we can't love others without first getting our hearts full of God's love. Once we harness God's nuclear energy within our relationship, then we are to give it away. Think about it: nuclear energy is a mighty force, but it's useless if the energy isn't used for something productive.

Earlier I noted that nuclear energy starts by rearranging uranium neutrons in a process called fission. Fission releases energy that can be used to make steam, and the steam can then be used to power a turbine to generate electricity.[14] A typical nuclear power plant supplies enough electricity to power 893,000 homes.[15] A nuclear generator the size of a hot tub can produce enough electricity to supply twenty thousand homes.[16] In the same way, the incredible spiritual energy between a husband and wife is unleashed. Don't keep this power bottled up!

Erin and I have found that developing shared dreams as a couple is like unleashing nuclear energy in and through our marriage. The nuclear math of marriage can be changed again: 1 + 1 = infinity.

Dreaming Together   200655

God unites couples to do together what they could never do alone. Genesis 2:24 explains this vital component of marriage: "A man leaves his father and mother and is joined to his wife, and the two are united into one" (NLT). This principle of unity is called *synergy*. Synergy is the cooperation of two or more elements to produce a combined effect greater than the sum of their separate effects.[17] Like nuclear energy, spiritual oneness is a powerful force.

I think God's words also apply to marriage and the power of working together toward a united goal. When a couple is united and working toward a shared vision, then nothing is impossible for husband and wife. I appreciate how Dr. Neil Clark Warren, founder of eHarmony, explains the synergy of dreaming together:

> Magnificent marriages involve two people who dream magnificently. The partners encourage each other to dig deeper and dream bigger, and in the process they get in touch with a level of being and doing that otherwise would be far beyond them.[18]

Dreaming "magnificently" isn't about creating common goals like buying a house, paying off school debt, having kids, or going on a particular vacation. These goals are important, but I'm talking about a bigger vision that enables God to use your marriage for *His* purpose. We've already looked at Ephesians 3:20, and there's another promise about the value of dreaming together in Scripture:

> Delight yourself in the LORD and he will give you the de-
> sires of your heart. Commit your way to the LORD; trust
> in him and he will do this. (Psalm 37:4-5)

When we dream together and ask God to use our marriage for His purpose, He unleashes nuclear energy through us and accomplishes something greater than we could have ever imagined.

To thrive, your marriage has to be about something bigger than individual gratification and the pursuit of pleasure, which is hedonism. Inwardly focused marriages do not fulfill the desires of God, and they die. I liken a marriage that is based only on meeting selfish needs to the Dead Sea. This salt-laden lake has but one major water source: the Jordan River. Because the Dead Sea has no outlets, the salt accumulates, killing all the fish and other creatures. Likewise, when you dam up your marriage, others can't be blessed by it. But if a couple commits to pursuing God's love and it flows through them and back into the community, God will give you your desires and more.

What Is Your Dream?

What or who is your vision? What is God calling you as a couple to do? Find a cause that you and your spouse are both passionate about—something that benefits others—and give yourselves to it. Maybe your shared dream is to . . .

- help married couples thrive (this is our newest dream together);
- mentor engaged or young married couples;
- lead a Bible study;
- spend time on a short-term mission trip;
- give significant amounts of money to ministries;

- work with troubled youth;
- lead a prayer ministry at your church;
- feed the homeless;
- sponsor a needy child;
- adopt a child;
- volunteer at church;
- teach a children's Bible class.

Whatever you both dream about doing together, others need to be blessed by your marriage. The fruit of your shared dream is that you are loving God by loving others. This promise is articulated with a beautiful analogy in the book of Jeremiah:

They are like trees planted along a riverbank, with roots that reach deep into the water. Such trees are not both-ered by the heat or worried by long months of drought. Their leaves stay green, and they never stop producing fruit. (17:8, NLT)

Robertson McQuilkin's love for his wife, Muriel, was evi-dent to all and blessed others. One day he and Muriel were at an airport and their flight was delayed two hours. McQuilkin pa-tiently answered his wife's repetitive questions about their delay, where they were, and when they would get home. A female onlooker wistfully commented that she hoped a man would one day love her as devotedly.[19]

Visit *crazylittlethingcalledmarriage.com* for free date night ideas that reflect the themes of this chapter. You'll also find complimentary discussion questions for all the Romance Secrets in this book.

In "Romance Secret #3," you'll discover that spiritual intimacy can be enhanced by good communication, "to know and be known."

TRUE LOVE STRIVES TO KNOW AND BE KNOWN

*Now we see but a poor reflection as in a
mirror; then we shall see face to face.
Now I know in part; then I shall know
fully, even as I am fully known.*
—1 Corinthians 13:12

I knew from the instant this couple walked into my office
that the husband and wife were estranged. The wife—thirty-
something years old—sat on the couch, set down her purse,
and smoothed her blouse. She looked around at the antique
sports equipment hanging on the walls in approval. Then she
offered me a halfhearted smile. But she never once glanced at
her husband.

The husband was in a gray suit as if just from the office.
Tentatively he sat on the other end of the couch, then he leaned
sideways toward his wife.

She turned her head away and lifted up her palm like a shield.

The man pivoted on the couch and faced me.

"Greg," he said, "things aren't so great at home. I can't figure her out. Maybe she'll talk to you."

I got the wife's attention and asked for her perspective.

"That man is never home," the wife began.

(Marriage Counseling 101 tip #1: it's not good when a wife calls her husband "that man.")

"That's not true!" the husband shouted.

(Marriage Counseling 101 tip #2: it's not good when couples shout at each other.)

The wife cut him an intimidating glance. "And when he is, he's doing something on the computer."

"A guy's got to work," he said.

She rolled her eyes. "There's golf on Tuesdays, Thursdays, and Saturdays. Racquetball on Fridays with the office guys. Monday he volunteers at the courthouse. Wednesday he's home, but he stays in the garage working on his hobbies and projects. Sundays are all filled with church activities and family."

Astute counselor that I am, I ventured, "So, communication's not that good."

The husband jumped up. "You can say that again." He turned toward his wife, pointing a finger, then shaking it in rage. "She won't even speak to me! Not. One. Word!" He flicked the finger with every syllable.

I gave her a quizzical look. "Is that true?"

The woman nodded.

"Why not?" I asked.

She shrugged and said, "Momma always told me, 'Never talk to strangers.'"

Unfortunately, that wasn't the opening to a sitcom about marriage woes. This exaggerated anecdote is based on a sad reality I see in real counseling situations: many couples don't know each other. They're roommates or business partners. It would be a lot less expensive for them if they learned to talk to one another without a counselor to mediate. And I'm not only referring to the cost of an office fee—there's also a high emotional price to be paid when spouses don't communicate well.

A 2013 survey of one hundred mental health professionals revealed the following:

- "Communication problems" was the most common complaint leading to divorce, followed by the "inability to resolve conflict" (65 and 43 percent, respectively).
- Seventy percent of men blamed nagging and/or complaining as the top contributing factor.
- A close second for men (60 percent) was a spouse "not expressing sufficient appreciation."
- Eighty-three percent of women noted that "a lack of validation for their feelings and opinions" contributed to divorce.
- Fifty-six percent blamed "their spouse not listening or talking about himself too much."[1]

THE MEDIA ROMANCE FORMULA

Couples in trouble often don't know how to communicate. They picked up bad habits somewhere—either from their families or from the culture. In literature and in the movies, couples often begin a relationship by offering each other insults or demeaning, witty one-liners—this was true even of characters in older works such as Beatrice and Benedick in Shakespeare's *Much Ado About Nothing* and Elizabeth Bennett and Fitzwilliam Darcy in Jane Austen's *Pride and Prejudice*. Those couples are so popular their quarrels are relived in modern performances. For example, Mr. Darcy has battled Lizzy in at least ten onscreen versions of *Pride and Prejudice* since 1938.[2]

**Grant that I may not so much seek to
be understood, as to understand.**

St. Francis of Assisi, "The Prayer of Saint Francis"

After the sparring wanes, miscommunication becomes the turning point of the romance plot. The mix-up leads to either comedy or drama—sometimes both. Who can forget the tension between big-city Melanie and the redneck husband who refuses to divorce her in *Sweet Home Alabama*? Or the not-so-well-kept secrets that spill out in movies such as *Twilight* ("Honey, I'm a vampire"), *Shrek* ("Honey, I'm an ogress"), or *What Women Want* ("Honey, I'm the guy who's sabotaging your marketing career"). And how about those two rival booksellers unknowingly engaged in an online romance in *You've Got Mail*?

The audience waits for the tender scene in which emotional vulnerabilities are offered—the significant piece of personal revelation that allows the lover-in-waiting to hope. Movies would like you to believe that a person has to lower his or her guard just once, then the couple has a brief emotional exchange, and voilà, love blossoms like cherry trees in spring!

At the movies, the onlookers cheer for the couple once they unite, because everything is now supposed to be perfect and all misconceptions are cleared up. The man and woman, once avowed of each other's love, will never have a moment of miscommunication; they'll instinctively think each other's thoughts. All the facades, emotional barriers, and pretentions are forever torn down. No more trust issues or fear. The man and woman will be in one accord in home decorating, theology, sleep habits, childrearing priorities, and, the largest hurdle: finances. And certainly no problems in the bedroom.

Those cultural concepts are not sustainable long-term. Quarreling breaks down trust and isolates couples. Self-revelation is not a one-time process like cracking an egg. You must continually peel away the onionskin of self, offering each layer to your spouse, even if it stings. If you try to communicate like the couples in a movie-made romance, you'll soon find yourself cast in a tragedy.

Don't try those communication techniques at home.

LETTING GO OF THE LIE

Then why is communicating with someone you love so difficult? Why does the human heart cling to the Hollywood lies and pay at the box office to see those myths perpetuated?

I believe it's because men and women were created for community, to be known intimately, to feel understood and still be desired. That's the true part. The fallacy is that communication is easy, a one-hundred-minute, full-color fix. Couples want the process to be effortless, and instead it's often the most difficult work they've ever faced.

You and your spouse will never be able to read each other's minds; however, you can know and be known intimately. This is *better* than reading minds because learning to know and be known forces us to become better spouses—and better people—in myriad ways.

> *Men and women were created for community, to be known intimately, to feel understood and still be desired.*

Once you've established that you're committed to God, your marriage, and to each other, a safe environment is built for trust and communication to deepen. Communication is what holds relationships together.

BLOOD AND MORTAR

Remember the home-temple example from Ephesians 2:19-22? Married couples share a temple for two, built on the cornerstone of Christ. As you picture that, mentally add building stones that are held fast by mortar. If the stones are loose, the home will not be up to code. Think of good communication as the mortar that keeps you close. Psychologist Amy Bellows commented:

> Communication is the mortar that holds a relationship together—if it breaks down, the relationship will crumble. When spouses no longer communicate, a marriage nurtures no one. It is no longer a marriage.[3]

Another way to look at good communication in marriage comes from the study of biology. Communication is the lifeblood of a marriage. Blood is responsible for supplying oxygen and transporting nutrients to the far regions of the body. It also fights off infection.

Without communication, a marriage will suffocate.

Without communication, a marriage will starve.

Without communication, disease will run rampant in your relationship.

Without the blood of healthy communication, your marriage is as lifeless as a statue of Elvis in a wax museum.

COUPLES COMMUNICATION

There's an entire field of psychology that studies gender differences, and the gaps in male-female communication in particular are given close scrutiny. In fact, even the gender definitions of the concept clash: Women define communication as opening their heart, delving deeply into feelings, and exploring thoughts and emotions with their spouse. Men see it as scratching out a short note before suddenly disappearing to go fishing with the boys.

The gender differences between men and women make communication challenging because, in general, members of each gender have their own goals. And those goals often conflict.

Men

Men usually have a specific conversation goal (notice the singularity of purpose). They typically utilize talking as purposeful action. In my experience, and others agree,[4] men use communication to get to the root of a problem as quickly as possible.

A husband might see little need to speak unless there is a specific intention behind it:

- a point that needs to be made
- a problem to solve
- a decision to make
- something that needs to be fixed

The masculine gender, as a rule, focuses on facts and seeks immediate resolutions. Men don't always like to make eye contact when talking and may prefer to walk beside their spouse or to sit in the car and talk where they are shoulder to shoulder. For many men, face-to-face conversation with eye contact is an adversarial posture, and it feels uncomfortable in a marriage relationship setting.[5]

Surprisingly, the stereotype of the talkative woman and the tight-lipped man isn't based on empirical data. Here's a synopsis of a thorough study by Dr. Matthias Mehl of the University of Arizona psychology department:

> On average, women speak 16,215 words per day and men speak 15,669 words per day . . . However, Dr. Mehl says that the mean is not the best descriptor of this distribution—the distribution for this study was huge. One person used an estimated 795 words on average per day . . . while another used almost 47,000 words (both the least and the most talkative participants were men). However, the distributions were normal for both sexes and averaged out to have no statistical difference.[6]

It really doesn't matter how many words other men speak per day or whether Mars and Venus have differing communication orbits. What does matter is that you and your spouse understand each other's preferred communication style. Men, plan to discuss with your wife the ways in which you feel most comfortable talking about relationship topics. Answer the following questions for starters:

- What makes you feel most comfortable while talking about important issues?
- Which settings are best: kitchen, bedroom, living room, outdoors, restaurants, or inside the car?
- What time of day: early, lunch, dinner, or later in the evening?
- Which timeframe is closest to your comfort zone for discussing personal issues: two minutes, twenty minutes, or two hours?
- How can your wife let you know that she has understood your viewpoints and preferences? This doesn't mean she agrees with you, but that she can explain your perspective.

Women

Women's goals for conversation are intimacy and connection (note the dual purposes).[7] They see conversation as an act of sharing, as a way to release negative feelings, and as an opportunity to increase intimacy with their husband.

Wives communicate for the following reasons:

- to discover how they are feeling and share the information
- to identify what it is they want to say
- to talk about problems extensively
- to find common experiences

The feminine talker loves to look deeply into her husband's eyes. Coffee shop conversations or chats at a small restaurant table are perfect for intimate conversation.[8]

Misfortunate Miscue

We were on our way to watch Garrison's basketball team play in a championship game on a Saturday afternoon. Everyone was loaded into our van, which has one of those keyless ignition switches where you simply push a button to start your vehicle.

PHONE ETIQUETTE

Do you love your cell phone? Fifty percent of Americans sleep with theirs near them; they're a cyber teddy bear of sorts.[9] Your cell phone can help you become a better spouse. Studies about cell phone use show that they can help couples maintain intimacy while they are apart. Here are a few findings based on studies of friendship in general and some on couples in particular:

Those who communicate via both face to face and electronic means rated higher levels of intimacy than those who communicate only face to face.[10] Bottom line, text and e-mail your spouse compliments and encouragement. Texting doesn't replace talking in person, but text messages bolster feelings of intimacy. Erin especially likes to save texts and reread them, which extends those loving feelings.

Be careful, though! It's difficult for me to think about Erin while I'm working, so I've taped a small note to my computer monitor that says, "Text Erin." This reminds me to connect with her during the workday. One day, after seeing my note, I started texting her. My first text started off pretty tame; I thanked her for cooking breakfast. Then I told her how beautiful she looked in the new outfit that she had put on and how

---

Since we had arrived ten minutes early, I dropped off the family in front of the gym. I then told Erin that I was going to drive down the street to the bank and make a deposit—I'd be killing two birds with one stone!

Erin tried to give me some instructions about the keyless ignition system and the fact that she couldn't find the remote. Honestly, I just wanted to get to the bank and back before the game started. So I really discounted her caution. I raced to the bank, turned the van off, and hustled inside.

cool it was that the kids were all going to be gone that evening. The next texts quickly went beyond a PG rating! I smiled as I hit the send button. It wasn't ten seconds later that I heard the familiar ding indicating I had received a text. As I started reading, I was horrified to see it was from my boss. Somehow I accidentally sent him the text. "Please tell me that your text message was meant for your wife" was all he wrote. I was humiliated. But to mess with him, I replied, "No . . . I was just thinking about our meeting later on today!"

If you're out of town, use the phone to contact your spouse and be attentive. That's better than texting or sending an email. Connecting by phone affirms feelings of commitment.[11]

It's wise to set parameters on response time. Don't expect your spouse to answer a text within five minutes; a two-hour turnaround—or longer depending on job constraints—is more realistic. Defining expectations can alleviate some disappointments and keep you closer.[12]

If you allow your spouse full access to your phone and contact list—no privacy boundaries—your marriage may be strengthened. And try using texts to administrate. It's an efficient use of time, so when you get face to face, you can talk about more important things.

Everything was working perfectly until I got back into the van and pushed the ignition button. Nothing! Instead of a mighty V-6 motor revving to life, all I got was a dashboard message that said, "Ignition key not recognized." Then it dawned on me that—just perhaps—this is what Erin was trying to tell me when I drove off in the middle of her instructions. I looked at my watch; it was about five minutes before tip-off!

My only real option was to lock up the van and start jogging. I instantly encountered several problems. Garrison's gym was more than a mile away, I was wearing flip-flops, and it had been about two years since I'd gone jogging!

Needless to say, I arrived at the basketball game late and sore. When I found Erin and the rest of my family, I was sweating profusely.

"Why are you so late?" Erin asked, smirking. "And I can only imagine why you are sweating?"

"I had to run all the way from the bank," I explained.

Erin seemed to instantly recognize the problem. "You turned off the ignition, didn't you?" she asked, smiling. "That's what I was trying to explain when you drove off."

In hindsight, I was so focused on getting my task completed in a hurry that I wasn't able to slow down and listen. Because Erin was annoyed that I devalued her advice, she wasn't invested enough to make sure I understood her.

Don't let this happen to you.

Wives, help your spouse understand your communication preferences by answering the list in the previous section, swapping out the word *wife* with *husband*.

LONG-DISTANCE LIMITS

It's good to set expectations on other forms of communication too. Early in our marriage, Erin would feel overwhelmed whenever I traveled. She was exhausted from keeping up with the house and small kids, so she would call me to vent. She'd say things such as, "You've been traveling too much," and "At least you got a full night's sleep!"

In those early days, I'd try to reason her out of her frustration. I'd say things such as, "We agreed to do this," "I don't have a choice—what do you want me to do?" and "I'm here, and it's not helping me to hear you complain." I was trying to condition her into a calm response, like training one of Pavlov's dogs. But Erin wasn't up for being conditioned. She was resisting my pleas as a cat would, which is to say flat-out ignoring my overtures for understanding.

One day our conversation got so heated, I hung up on her. That didn't go over well.

Eventually I called her back, and she said my comments left her feeling invalidated. She explained that she didn't need me to "fix it" or justify myself—she just needed to talk to someone about how difficult things were when she was alone.

So I listened. And I listened some more. Over the months, my listening did nothing to help her or me. I felt helpless—trapped between my job responsibilities and my family ones. I didn't see any purpose to the calls, and they were draining me emotionally at a time when I needed to stay energized for my audience.

Finally I began to say things like this: "You deserve to have me look you in the eyes, so we need to work this out when I get home, when we can be face to face. I love you, and we're on the same team." We slowly turned the long-distance communication corner.

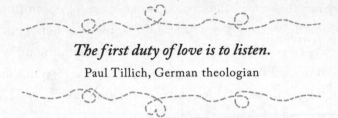

The first duty of love is to listen.
Paul Tillich, German theologian

Now we've learned that those phone calls and Skype appointments should be about pursuing each other emotionally and bolstering the relationship. We leave problem solving and venting for a time when I'm home and we can actually come to satisfying agreements.

A IN ADMINISTRATION, F IN RELATIONSHIP

Coming to terms with technology will always be an issue—especially since we Americans are administrators and our gadgets help us. (Soon there will be an app to translate from male to female and back again.)

But think about it. Cell phones are loaded with the ultimate administration apps to coordinate calendars, carpools, and credit card accounts. Couples all over the world stuff their life information into a tiny computer to prioritize and manage their time.

Then, when couples sit down to have a conversation with their spouses, they administrate their marriages almost to death. They discuss the house, work, the kids, school, shopping, budgeting, car maintenance, elder care, church, doctor appointments, vacations . . .

This is a huge problem for the couples I counsel. Erin and I are not immune. We continually battle against letting administration overtake our time together. At night, instead of asking the important questions, such as how this day went or how the events affected us, we sometimes plan the next day's activities. If we let administration run rampant, we run into trouble.

For men, this type of administrative, facts-based communication fits with their purpose-driven communication style. For women, the organized and praised Proverbs 31 woman is in her glory, talking about her vast responsibilities and how to accomplish them. In the workplace or other task-centered places, this transactional style of communication works well. And, in fact, marriages need administrative communication. Real and practical concerns press down on every couple.

> *If we let administration run rampant, we run into trouble.*

But when marriages get stuck in administration, it's like mixing too much sand into the communication mortar, causing it to crumble. If you are content with the impersonal nature of your discussions, you might as well be married to an overseas administrative assistant you hired via the Internet.

Right now, Erin is planning a trip to China and taking our two oldest daughters with her. That will leave me with a book manuscript deadline, two kids who need a chauffeur, and a whole lot of appointments because it's back-to-school time. Erin and I are being pulled into an administrative vortex. And if we're not careful, we won't be able to share the hopes and expectations we had for this special graduation/birthday trip for the girls. We'll be more concerned with speech-therapy appointments and who is going to bring our youngest daughter home from school every day than how our fears, dreams, and spiritual lives are driving our emotions and actions.

What can we do?

Erin and I have developed habits—almost rituals—that push us past the administration and into the heart of the issues.

Now Hear This!

The first habit we learned was to listen. In the third century BC, Greek historian Diogenes came up with a helpful observation. He humorously pointed out that, "We have two ears and only one mouth so that we would listen the more and talk the less."[13]

Despite the numerical advantage, the ears of married couples are often off duty. When you do carve out time for real conversation, be careful none of it is lost. Disagreements and conflict result from lost information (and we'll discuss those at length in the next chapter), but poor listening also creates emotional distance. If communication ceases, if you share your soul and don't feel heard, isolation fills the silence and the relationship cools in the emotional vacuum.

The best way—the only way—for you to make sure you've heard your spouse (and this isn't rocket science) is to repeat what he or she has told you. Psychologists call it *reflection*. And, yes, until you get the hang of it, the words spill out awkwardly, like your tongue feels after you've bitten it too hard. Initially you'll feel a bit patronizing, perhaps even like an imbecile. But here's what one leadership expert tells students who complain that repeating sounds phony:

> Skilled listeners know that tactfully showing that you
> have heard what someone has said by reflecting it back
> to them requires creativity, and they've had to practice

creative paraphrasing and reflecting to become good at it. Yes, the process of learning how to use reflecting can be awkward for people who are inexperienced with it. However, be very careful not to avoid practicing and learning a skill just because you're concerned that you will not immediately be proficient. It's better to develop communication skills over time, despite the possible awkward stage, than to completely avoid developing those skills due to a fear of the initial awkwardness.[14]

A little awkwardness (okay, *more* than a little sometimes) is worth it in order to hear the heart of your loved one. You'll find it even helps with simple activities like getting to the school play on time or remembering your spouse's bowling shoe size.

CULTIVATE A SAFE ENVIRONMENT

Another communication habit we've developed is creating emotional safety. This process is essential to maintaining open communication. This goes well beyond putting the cell phone away and looking your spouse in the eyes to establish connection. It means your spouse feels free to open up and reveal who he or she really is—to share his or her deepest feelings, thoughts, hopes, and dreams. And you know that your spouse will listen, understand, validate, and unconditionally accept you.

Avoid Value Judgments
One way to create this safe environment is to avoid making value judgments. Here's how *not* to respond . . .

A man I know had an argument with his wife every Saturday

morning around 8:30. After the trashcans were emptied by the city garbage collectors, the wife, Isabel, would want them dragged back behind the fence. And she wanted it done "right now."

Grant, the husband, wanted to sleep in and "connect" with his wife on the lazy weekend mornings. Having either one of them rise and shine to hide the garbage cans spoiled the mood.

Their arguments moved from ridicule to insults.

He said: "What's the big deal if the cans stay on the curb an extra hour? I can't believe you let a little thing like that bother you."

She said: "Why can't you just get up and move them? I knew you didn't care about me."

He said: "Now you're just being ridiculous."

She said: "You're so insensitive."

And so on.

The problem was that Isabel valued having her home look neat and tidy; it reflected on her personally. Those ugly, empty trashcans sitting by the street made her feel shame, as if she were disrespecting the neighbors. Grant was left feeling rejected and unloved. He couldn't imagine why moving those trashcans was more important to Isabel than spending time with him.

They did have to move the trashcans, but the arguments about it were out of control and left emotional garbage that wasn't so easy to dispose of.

To create a safe space, avoid "judging" your spouse's thoughts, feelings and opinions. Don't say things like . . .

- You're so sensitive.
- Your feelings are wrong.
- That's ridiculous. You shouldn't feel that way.

- It's no big deal. Why do you get so emotional?
- It's just your time of the month!
- Lighten up. You're overreacting.
- You're so dramatic. Your emotions are out of control.
- You're crazy! That's not how you really feel.
- Can't you take a joke?
- Relax. Stop freaking out!
- You are not being very rational.
- It's nothing to get upset over. You shouldn't let it bother you.
- You should be over that by now.

Validate

Instead of judging your spouse, communicate that his or her heart and emotions are important to you, regardless of whether you agree or they make sense. When you validate your spouse, you respect, value, and accept your spouse's heart—his or her deep thoughts, opinions, ideas, beliefs, and emotions. Validation creates emotional safety.

Grant could have said, "I know it's important to you to have a nice home. I respect your desire to fit in with the neighbors. But it's important to me to have uninterrupted time with you, and we get so little of it. I love you and desire to be near you."

Validation creates emotional safety.

Isabel could have said, "I love you and appreciate that you work hard and want to unwind on Saturdays. It means a lot to me that you value our private time together when we're not stressed. But I'm distracted by the responsibility to move the trashcans, and it's not easy to relax if they're out there."

Instead of insulting, which comes all too easily, try saying things like . . .

- Your feelings are important to me, but I honestly need your help to understand them.
- Can you explain where your feelings are coming from?
- I can see you're upset. This is a big deal to you.
- You seem more agitated than the problem calls for. Is everything okay?

ERIN AS VALIDATE-ATORIAN

I really wanted validation from Greg when we first got married. When he didn't tell me what I was feeling was okay, I would get stuck in the "what's wrong with me?" vortex. He didn't like being criticized, and anger frightened him, which was unfortunate because this cycle typically triggered it. As a result of my tears and heated emotion, he would shut down and not communicate at all.

My parents never discussed emotions, so I hadn't learned how to talk about them. When I tried revealing my inner life, my parents tended to question me or shut me down. At least that's what I see when looking back on it.

One time in high school, for example, I got into an argument with my best friend. I felt as if our relationship completely disintegrated in those few minutes. I came home upset and feeling the loss. I turned to my parents for support. Unable to process my sorrow, they raised questions about what I had done to cause the breach. That was not helpful, and afterward it left me hesitant to talk about my feelings at all.

During our first year of marriage, I went to counseling

- Can you help me understand why you're so upset?
- Your feelings aren't making sense to me. I'm sorry if
  I made light of them.
- That happened a long time ago. It must have hurt
  a lot since it still bothers you.

This type of communication opens the door for the true heart to be seen, imperfections and all. Without knowing the difficult stuff, the work-in-progress information about your spouse, you can't really know him or her at all.

and learned that my feelings were important—the "voice of my heart." After that I had new confidence, so even if Greg didn't acknowledge my emotions, I wouldn't psychologically crumble. Instead I stood up for myself. Because Greg had the Smalley marriage background, at first I believed I was one-hundred-percent responsible for our marriage problems. After counseling I could push back on Greg, and he began to be more interested in what was going on in my internal life.

I also learned to be less critical of my new husband and to acknowledge that Greg's personality was different from mine. A lot of what Greg does is spur-of-the-moment. He lives in the "now." So I learned that just because he didn't plan or organize, it wasn't up to me to do all the chores and figure out how to pay the bills. His intention was to have fun—something that drew me to him in the first place and is still one of the most appealing parts of his personality. After a year or so, I changed my mindset; we were able to communicate deep feelings, emotions, thoughts, and motivations. That's one of the ways we turned the corner and began to enjoy marriage—rekindling those romantic feelings—instead of merely enduring it.

KNOW AND BE KNOWN

Being known thoroughly is what Christian relationships are about—that's the whole point of communication. Marriage is modeled after the relationship of Jesus and the Father. Here's how Jesus describes it:

> I no longer call you servants, because a servant does not know his master's business. Instead, I have called you friends, for everything that I learned from my Father I have made known to you. (John 15:15)

First, you have to move into Jesus' inner circle. You're no longer on the outside—you can "know" God incarnate. In the same way, you can move into your spouse's life and know him or her intimately. You're in the inner circle.

From day one, I've been mesmerized by Erin—by her femininity, her smile, her likes, her commitment to God, her career. More than two decades later, I still feel surprised by her wonderfulness. I will continue to fuel my curiosity about her and seek to know her better every day.

Too often husbands and wives are afraid to put their feelings and thoughts into words

In "Romance Secret #5: True Love Honors," we'll talk more about how to rediscover your true love and stay current by regularly updating your knowledge of your spouse. There is great joy in rediscovering aspects of your mate's heart and mind.

In "Romance Secret #11: True Love Looks Inward," the value of being known by your spouse will be addressed. For now it's enough to realize that part of committing to marriage means to offer yourself and to be vulnerable. Too often husbands and wives are afraid to put their feelings and thoughts into words and have them evaluated, perhaps unkindly.

This process of self-revelation—peeling away the onion of self—can be particularly painful, especially if you had difficult experiences in the past, or if you learned to be reserved as you watched your parents and peers. Express your thoughts and feelings fully. Share your thoughts and feelings with your spouse as well.

Be Fully Known

A couple of years ago, I went on a road trip with two of my friends from college (let's call them Frank and Geoff). As the miles flew by, we also caught up on the milestones in each other's lives. Suddenly, Frank started a conversation about affairs. He was riding shotgun, turned to me, and asked point-blank: "Greg, have you ever had an affair?"

I answered, "No, man. I take my wife or a family member with me whenever I travel. I don't want that to happen to me."

Frank turned all the way around to face Geoff, who was sitting in the back seat. "What about you?" Frank asked. "Have you ever had an affair?"

A strange and awkward silence rode along with us for the rest of the trip.

Later Geoff and I discussed his affair, which was far in the past. I was the first person he'd ever told. I encouraged him to tell his wife.

Of course, Geoff's first reactions to my suggestion were jumbled: He wanted to let sleeping dogs lie—in Vegas if at all possible. He didn't want to hurt his wife, even though he knew he already had. He wanted to avoid poking a hornet's nest, to not ask and to not tell. He wanted to cover up and hide his Bathsheba debacle. But Geoff also knew the principle in Luke 12:2, "There is nothing concealed that will not be disclosed, or hidden that will not be made known."

Everything about a healthy marital union on this earthly plane has been designed by God to be a reflection of the interaction that we are meant to have with God Himself.

David Kyle Foster, *The Divine Marriage*

Geoff decided to come clean, which allowed his wife to know what had previously been concealed. As you can imagine, the process was as close to emotional torture as you can get without a water bucket. But Geoff recently told me that he and his wife are emotionally and spiritually closer. She was able to forgive, to reconcile. And they now know each other more intimately than ever before.

I mentioned that communication is like blood. Sometimes you have to bleed a bit to be understood, to be fully known. There's an old saying that sums it up well: "It is sometimes essential for a husband and a wife to quarrel—they get to know each other better."[15] This idea leads us into the next relationship tool, "Romance Secret #4: True Love Fights for Peace."

Be sure to visit *crazylittlethingcalledmarriage.com* for date night ideas.

TRUE LOVE FIGHTS FOR PEACE

For as churning the milk produces butter,
and as twisting the nose produces blood,
so stirring up anger produces strife.
—Proverbs 30:33

Remember the last day of our Hawaiian honeymoon? Erin and I were at a secluded beautiful waterfall, and she wouldn't join me in the water. My words, "You've just ruined the honeymoon," wrenched Erin's heart. That's when Hurricane O (Our First Fight) blew in.

As promised, here's her version of the storm:

The NO SWIMMING sign posted near the water meant nothing to him. In his world of perpetual fun and adventure, caution signs like that don't exist, and if they do, they're ignored.

First, I'm a nurse, and following rules is something nursing school drills into you. A NO SWIMMING sign means just that: NO SWIMMING. All sorts of health risks could have been lurking in that water: leeches, pathogenic protozoa, piranhas.

Second, I'm a person who thinks through my actions. What if by swimming we were disturbing the breeding ground of some rare fish or an endangered salamander? What if the area was off limits because too many swimmers had already compromised the ecosystem?

And I respect other people's property. What if this waterfall and pond were on private property, and the owner just didn't want people swimming there? That's enough reason for me.

So when Greg heaped the blame on, I turned away and hiked back to civilized company.

This was one of the worst moments of our honeymoon. But it could have been one of the best in terms of building lasting intimacy. Why? Because it was a perfect learning situation.

RELATIONSHIP FRICTION + INSIGHT =

INTIMACY INFORMATION

INTIMACY INFORMATION + HEALTHY COMMUNICATION =

HAPPY MARRIAGE

It's another one of those crazy principles of marriage that on the surface doesn't make sense. In fact, the culture tells us that fighting in a marriage is a sign that true love has left town.

But if Erin and I had been smart (insight) and talked about (healthy communication) why we both overreacted (relationship friction), we would have been healthier (happy marriage) and spared ourselves dozens of sarcasm-slinging scenarios in the months to come.

Looking back, I now see I could have gained insight about Erin's integrity and her wisdom. She would have come to appreciate my efforts at working recreation into our lives and my ability to organize and plan special moments.

In the short term, conflict is painful and points to the fact that you don't always understand your spouse or yourself. But if you know how to break the conflict code, you'll be better able

---

IF MAMA AND PAPA AIN'T HAPPY

To have a thriving romantic relationship, you'll need to identify your own style of conflict engagement, which you may have learned from your parents, consciously or unconsciously. Did they fight, tossing insults like grenades? Were they never able to get close, like two soldiers with bayonets raised? Or perhaps they avoided conflict altogether like a submarine silently passing below a naval battleship. Did they merely share the budget and little else, one living a life in boardrooms and the other in the trenches at home?

Many of you watched your parents disappear behind closed doors to argue, so you don't have the foggiest idea how they worked through their problems. But none of their bad patterns need to keep you from choosing a different style of conflict resolution.

You can create a new plan for *your* family. You have the opportunity to use conflict—those times when you're hurt, annoyed, frustrated, wounded, confused, angry, and discouraged with one another—to grow closer together.

not only to avoid the next flare-up but also head it off at the pass and earn points in the romance department.

In the long term, you can expect conflicts and prepare for them when they "come your way" as the book of James advises:

> Dear brothers and sisters, when troubles of any kind
> come your way, consider it an opportunity for great joy.
> For you know that when your faith is tested, your endur-
> ance has a chance to grow. So let it grow, for when your
> endurance is fully developed, you will be perfect and
> complete, needing nothing. (1:2-4, NLT)

While most of us wouldn't consider relationship friction as a joyful "opportunity," successfully resolving a conflict *will* produce a happier marriage. You're never going to like conflict, but you'll like it better than perpetual discord.

CONFLICT VERSUS COMBAT:
RULES OF ENGAGEMENT

Learning the difference between handling a conflict well and engaging in emotional combat is essential to having a healthy marriage. This means learning to settle your differences in negotiations rather than through guerilla warfare.

Erin and I believe that after your relationship with the Lord, this is one of the most important aspects of preparing for a satisfying, lifelong marriage with the flames of passion and romance never subsiding. It's imperative that you learn how to face your differences and work through your disagreements and hurt. This requires a different mindset from winning or losing an argument—but it is still painful in the short term.

If you don't know how to reconcile conflicts through negotiations, combat will take over and ultimately ruin your marriage. Some of the best marriage researchers can even predict with a high degree of certainty if a marriage will succeed or fail simply based on how a couple deals with conflict. If the spouses argue without ever resolving their issues or consistently avoid conflict altogether, their marriage is at risk for divorce.[1] The apostle Paul recognized this same truth when he instructed the church at Galatia, "If you keep on biting and devouring each other, watch out or you will be destroyed by each other" (Galatians 5:15).

It's not how many arguments you have, it's how you manage them that makes all the difference. The goal is never to avoid your problems and keep peace at any price. It's making restitution, and seeking favor with your spouse. Look out for your spouse's needs first—and don't delay!

> *It's not how many arguments you have, it's how you manage them that makes all the difference.*

When Erin and I had our first fights, we avoided the underlying conflict. That bad habit led to a pain far deeper than the pain of arguing it out till we reconciled. It took us many months to finally get to the root of Hurricane O. We lost a lot of emotional blood along the way because the relationship wounds hadn't been cleaned and dressed.

WHY DO WE FIGHT IN THE FIRST PLACE?

The apostle James answered that question by writing, "What causes fights and quarrels among you? Don't they come from your desires that battle within you?" (James 4:1).

As in our story about Hurricane O, arguments are rarely

really about the surface issue (money, household chores, children, sex, work, leisure time, in-laws, whether to swim, etc.). These topics appear to be what's driving the conflict, but they're an illusion. They are about internal issues that "battle within you."

At the Smalley house whenever someone lashes out in anger, we say our "button" got pushed. I'm sure you've heard the expression, "He just pushed my button" or "She is totally pushing my buttons." Another expression refers to a light switch, meaning you suddenly change emotions: "He flipped my switch."

Yet another way to explain the "desires within" is to liken them to a computer pop-up or launching an app that takes control of your computer for a while. Once the keyboard is struck or the mouse is clicked, you can't stop the program until it has run its course.

All people are prone to emotional pop-ups. They're the viruses in our psyche, the reactions that launch when you're overly sensitive, tired, or full of anger and frustration. Your behavior is suddenly rewired by a conversation, experience, set of circumstances, or a single event. In the moment, it's as if you were reprogrammed by an outside force, something that controlled you against your reason. And later, sometimes even in seconds, your heart locks up, leaving you emotionally drained of power.

> *Emotional pop-ups represent deep-seated, sensitive emotions that are easily triggered, seemingly from nowhere.*

To be clear, I'm not referring to simple feelings like being mad, depressed, annoyed, worried, upset, jealous, or bored. Emotional pop-ups represent deep-seated, sensitive emotions that are easily triggered, seemingly from nowhere. Some hacker planted the app, and it's activated without your conscious consent.

A pop-up is feeling . . .

- unloved
- disrespected
- rejected
- failed
- controlled
- abandoned
- inadequate
- devalued
- worthless
- not good enough
- invalidated
- unimportant
- misunderstood

The feelings in this list, and other emotions like them, are the "desires that battle within you" that cause conflict in a marriage. These emotional pop-ups cause the ongoing strife, not the day-to-day squabbles over money, chores, in-laws, or directions that drive conflict.

And, once this pop-up app is launched, your heart closes instantly. Let's look at the consequences when that happens.

Clamming Up Versus Mortal Combat

To *clam up* means to be secretive or shut tight. When a clam closes up, it tightens its muscle at the base of its shell to protect its heart. To open, a clam must feel safe enough to relax the muscle.

Keep that image of a clam in mind as we consider the closing-up or shutting-down process of the heart—an important key to understanding conflict. Over time, if a couple continues to practice unhealthy conflict, their closed hearts will eventually die to each other. A heart, like a clam, must be open to let in emotional nutrients. So clamming up can ultimately kill a marriage.

On the flip side is death by mortal combat, the "death" occurring when a heart gives out after experiencing too much battle.

Combat in marriage is just plain wrong. It's like that classic childhood debate: Who would win in a fight—Batman or Superman? Maybe you've even seen the trailer for a movie based on that very premise. Batman and Superman are supposed be on the same side, but somehow in the movie, the superheroes can't see it. One voice of reason is Alfred, Bruce Wayne's sage butler. He says to his employer, "You're going to go to war. [Superman] is not our enemy."[2] But Batman can't hear it because of past pain and hurt.

> *Many marriages would be better if the husband and the wife clearly understood that they are on the same side.*
>
> Zig Ziglar, motivational speaker and author

In marriage, when conflict turns to combat, no one wins. Instead of planning and strategizing how to get what you want from your spouse, remember there's always collateral damage (just like the destruction that happens when superheroes do battle). Unfortunately, a Fighter leaves behind a wounded spouse, every time.

Fighters are those who jump right into a conflict discussion and advocate for their own opinion, viewpoint, or perspective. Thus, Fighters spend the majority of their time in persuasion mode—defending their point of view. The problem with this reaction style is that it always sends the same message: I'm not safe for any meaningful interaction with you.

On the opposite end of the scale are the *Flighters*. Instead of engaging head-on, they emotionally disconnect because of their closed hearts. The film trailer shows Superman initially disappearing from public view, confused that even though he has just saved the world, politicians are questioning his motives. Like Superman, Flighters "fly" to avoid conflict or withdraw when the conversation becomes difficult.

The key trait of a Flighter is a reluctance to get into a disagreement (avoidance) or to stay with an important conversation (withdrawal). Flighters work hard to minimize conflict and believe there is little gain from getting upset. Their motto is "relax—problems have a way of working themselves out."

In avoidance mode, Flighters may use the phrase "agree to disagree" time and time again—which means they avoid conversations they think will end in conflict. A person who chooses to disengage always sends the same message: I'm disconnecting from any meaningful interaction with you.

Whether your style is fight or flight, nothing good will ever come from unhealthy conflict because it's the exact opposite of

> *Flighters work hard to minimize conflict and believe there is little gain from getting upset.*

love. Whereas love is patient, kind, content, humble, polite, selfless, calm, and grateful, closed-heartedness generates negative reactions that drive you both apart. Sadly, when your heart is closed, God's love is no longer flowing between you. And this is exactly where Satan wants you: loveless, disconnected and isolated.

So, instead of staying in reaction mode when we experience conflict, how do we use the disagreement to drive us into the deepest levels of intimacy and connection? We promise it's possible!

MANAGING CONFLICT IN HEALTHY WAYS

Think about the last time you were hurt or frustrated with your spouse, a time when your buttons were pushed, a pop-up flashed, your heart was closed and you were in reaction mode (fight or flight). Now, when you were in that state, when were you genuinely able to have a good, productive, Christ-like conversation with your spouse? Most people answer with a resounding, "Never!"

It's almost physically impossible to compromise when you're stirred up emotionally, your heart is closed and you're reacting. Your heart races, your blood pressure rises, and rational thoughts are no longer possible. So how do you get your heart open again?

Over the years, we have found three simple steps that help us open our hearts and manage conflict in a healthy way.

1. Call a Time-Out

Instead of continuing to argue and debate the situation, hit the pause button. In other words, get away from each other for a brief amount of time in order to de-escalate your stirred-up emotions. This is exactly what King Solomon wrote: "A fool gives full vent to his anger, but a wise man keeps himself under control" (Proverbs 29:11). Instead of continuing to react (fight or flight), you want to calm down.

Some of the things that can help to de-escalate your pushed

buttons and emotional pop-ups include taking some deep breaths of air, exercising, taking a walk, cleaning the house, listening to music, praying, journaling your feelings, and so on. The key is to create some space from each other and do something that will calm you down.

In the next chapter, we'll look at one of my parents' fights in detail. For now it's enough to know that when my dad is frustrated with my mom, he goes to his study to unwind. There he keeps some reminders on why marriage is important. He knows he has to cleanse his emotional palate and chew on the positive rather than feed his anger.

As you create some space, make sure to let your spouse know you're taking a time-out to get your heart back open. Tell him or her you'll be back later to finish the discussion. This is not "withdrawing."

Withdrawal is an extremely deadly "flight" reaction. Calling a time-out communicates you just need a short break in order to continue the conversation. The research suggests you might need at least twenty minutes to calm down after your buttons have been pushed or a pop-up takes over.

In the Smalley house, we have made it a rule that the person who calls the time-out should also be the one to initiate getting back together to talk about the conflict—but only when both hearts are open.

2. Identify Your Emotions

When we're hurt and frustrated, our thoughts are racing with what the other person did or didn't do. This is called *stewing*. We can't stop stewing about how much we were wronged or mistreated. If we continue to think about those issues, we will stay angry.

Remember Matthew 7:3: "Why do you look at the speck of sawdust in your brother's eye and pay no attention to the plank in your own eye?" If you're going to get your heart open, you have to shift from thinking about your "brother," which in this case is your spouse, to focusing on you. The way to make this important shift is to do what King David suggested: "In your anger do not sin; when you are on your beds, search your hearts and be silent" (Psalm 4:4).

While you are in your time-out, start focusing on your emotions—the voice of your heart. Ask yourself, "What button just got pushed?" Or "How did that pop-up open?" You want to name the button—identify the emotion, gather intimacy information to share. This will continue to calm you down and open your heart.

You might be thinking, *Whatever, Greg! Are you going to give me the chart with the little emoticons showing everything from sad to enraged enough to sleep on the couch forever? If I point to a frowny face will you give me a lollipop?*

I promise I am not patronizing you! Research done at UCLA shows that simply naming what you are feeling will cause your brain activity to shift from the amygdala—your fight or flight center—to a much more rational part of the brain: the prefrontal cortex. [3]

Simply naming emotions not only begins to impact the state of your closed heart, but it also impacts what is going on in your body physiologically.

Feelings are intimacy information. Emotions are neither right nor wrong, good or bad; they're just really helpful pieces of information. When a warning light goes off on your car's dashboard, it's a good idea to figure out what it means. In the same way, God created your emotions to function like your car's warning lights. When you're feeling something or a button has been pushed, it's a source of great information. The amazing part is how simply putting a name to your emotions calms you down.

Armed with improved clarity about your emotions, now you're ready for the final step.

3. Discover the Truth

Two of the biggest mistakes people make with their emotions is either to ignore them or to act upon them. Remember, emotions represent nothing more than information. But we should never mindlessly act upon any information without evaluating it first.

The best way to evaluate your emotions or feelings (the buttons or pop-ups) is to take that information to the Lord. You are searching for His truth about you and your spouse. If we try to determine the validity of our emotions and thoughts about our spouse, we are at risk for believing lies.

I love how King David was honest about his emotions and talked to God about how he was feeling—the good, the bad and the ugly. Just one example is when David cried, "My God, my God, why have you forsaken me? Why are you so far from saving me, so far from my cries of anguish?" (Psalm 22:1, NIV 2011). Those powerful emotions show that the shepherd-turned-king wasn't afraid to be honest with God about his feelings.

I want to be like David, a man after God's own heart, and manage my emotions by talking to God. When you experience emotions, the best thing you can do is to hold these feelings up to God's light. Take your emotions to God in order to discover His truth about how you feel. When dealing with difficult or painful emotions that surface during an argument, the worst choice is to accept your feelings as "truth." Feelings represent great intimacy information, but emotions on their own don't equal truth.

> *Love means loving the*
> *unlovable—or it is no virtue at all.*
> G. K. Chesterton, *Heretics*

For me, Satan's lies often led me to see Erin as a disrespectful and unappreciative wife. I don't want to trust my own interpretations and perceptions of what my wife does; I want God's perspective because ultimately He is the Source of truth. When my heart is closed, my view becomes distorted. I lack God's insight, wisdom, and truth. Ephesians 4:18 speaks to this point: "They are darkened in their understanding and separated from the life of God because of the ignorance that is in them due to the hardening of their hearts."

Discovering truth is all about abandoning your own conclusions regarding your spouse and pursuing God's truth. The great news is that God is so faithful. He only wants what's best for you and your spouse, and He is committed to restoring unity. God will give you a peace that surpasses all understanding about your emotions and will help you see the truth about your spouse.[4]

A WASH-OUT ARGUMENT

Next, I'm going to take those three steps and show you a Smalley family conflict resolution in action.

A few years ago, Erin asked me to help her clean the house. As an alternative, I offered to wash our vehicles with the kids in the driveway.

I said, "Just save me a room or two, and I'll get to it when I'm done with the kids." In hindsight, there may have been a better way to negotiate her request! I was about to strike out big time.

The kids and I had a blast washing the cars. While Erin was inside slaving away with the vacuum, we were outside having a massive water fight that led us to get out a huge blow-up water slide.

Meanwhile, our youngest daughter, Annie, was splashing me from her plastic kiddy pool. Though Erin had asked me to put her in a swimming diaper, Annie seemed fine without it. Until it was clear she wasn't. I sent her inside for a diaper change. And Erin sent Annie right back out for me to take care of the mess.

"Erin," I shouted, "Can't you change her real quick? You're already inside" (Strike 1.)

The back door flew open, and Erin said, "Her swimming suit is full of poop! This is why I asked you to put her swim diaper on."

"I didn't think she really needed a swim diaper." I defended myself. "Plus the diaper was in the house, and I was already outside." (Strike 2.)

Although she didn't even need to use words, her look clearly communicated, *Brilliant plan, genius! It appears like that really worked out well for you!*

Actually what Erin did say was, "If you had helped me clean like I'd asked, this wouldn't have happened."

"I'm not one of your children," I shot back. "You can't tell me to clean on your schedule. I said I would help when I was done washing the cars." (It's amazing how much I actually sounded like a kid.)

"So, explain then why you're just standing there watching the kids play on the slide," Erin argued. "Is this part of the deluxe car-wash package?" (Strike 3 . . . I was out!)

Here's how we resolved this conflict.

We Called a Time-Out

Erin and I were both clearly stirred up and tired. We had just arrived home from China with Annie and were exhausted. From that point on, nothing we could say or do would make a difference. We needed to get out of our reactive dance! Thankfully, Erin had the presence of mind to say, "I'm really upset right now, so I'm going back inside. I'll let you know when I'm ready to talk about what just happened." In essence, she called a time-out.

Honestly, I didn't want to take a break. I wanted to resolve the problem and reconnect. I hate when we're disconnected, and I hate being annoyed at my wife. But, I've also learned that forcing Erin into a conversation when one or both of us has a closed heart is a complete waste of time. Although I don't like it, I now understand the value of a relational time-out; it gives me time to get my heart open so we can talk in a healthy manner.

We Identified Our Feelings

After Erin announced she was going back inside, I just sat in the front yard watching the kids play on the water slide.

As I changed Annie into a clean diaper, my mind churned with negative thoughts about Erin: *Why was cleaning the house more important than having fun with the kids? Why couldn't Erin just play with us first and then all of us clean together? Why does she always yell at me when she doesn't get her way? She'll never change!*

Inside the house, Erin was also stewing. As she angrily ran the vacuum across the carpet, her mind raced with negative thoughts about me: *Why won't Greg help me with the housework? Why do I always need to be the responsible parent while he gets to be the fun parent? Why is it solely my responsibility to clean the house and change Annie? He never helps out . . . I feel alone!*

It's in these moments that I'm reminded about spiritual warfare. When my heart is closed, I'm upset with my wife, and Satan attacks my thoughts. He is the father of lies.[5] The attack is very subtle and the thoughts seem right in my mind. However, the tip-off that something is not right is when my thoughts become extreme.

As I sat there deep in thought, staring at my kids play on the water, I realized I was being attacked when I started to think things like *She'll never change!* and *She always yells!* Over the years I've learned to instantly pray when I sense I'm under attack (which is almost guaranteed when we're fighting). My prayer that day was based on Philippians 4:7-8. It went something like this: *God guard my heart and my mind right now . . . give me Your peace that surpasses all understanding. Help me recognize what is true, honorable, right, pure, lovely, admirable, excellent and praiseworthy about my wife and our marriage.*

> *Although I don't like it, I now understand the value of a relational time-out.*

The prayer instantly calmed me down and gave me God's perspective. Nothing was fixed or resolved regarding what we'd been arguing about, but at least the spiritual attack was over. Next I needed to shift my thoughts away from Erin and figure out what was really going on for me.

I quickly realized the deeper emotions that were driving the argument for me. I was feeling controlled and disrespected. When Erin wanted me to clean the house before washing the car, I felt as if she was trying to control and manipulate me into her schedule. What I wanted to do (wash the cars with the kids) didn't seem to matter. She wanted the chores done on her timeframe. I also felt her sarcastic comments were disrespectful.

> *But I believe we grow our relationships*
> *by reconciling our differences. That's how*
> *we become more loving people and truly*
> *experience the fruits of marriage.*
>
> Dr. John Gottman, *Why Marriages Succeed or Fail*

Putting a name to what I was feeling helped me calm down. Naming my emotions—*controlled* and *disrespected*—de-escalated the situation for me. Real change happened after I had that conversation with God about my feelings.

Meanwhile, inside the house, Erin was feeling alone. She felt deserted and that our household responsibilities were falling solely on her shoulders—as many things had lately with all the stress of Annie's coming home. To her, the marriage felt one-sided and that we weren't being a team.

We Discovered the Truth

Sitting next to my children playing on the water slide, I started praying. "God, what is true about how I feel? What is true about my wife? Is the truth that Erin is controlling? Is she disrespectful?"

I know when I've encountered God's truth compared to Satan's lies. God's truth will always provide peace. Satan's lies will always produce strife and discontentment. I quickly felt a peace that Erin wasn't a controlling, disrespectful wife. Now I needed to talk to her.

We Talked with Open Hearts

The next step was an honest conversation with Erin to find out what her perspective was and to explain my viewpoint.

The key to having a reconciling conversation is to make sure your heart is open to God's love, which is patient, kind, humble, honoring, sacrificial, self-controlled, and forgiving.[6] These are the exact attributes I needed for a healthy, productive conversation with Erin. But I had to open my heart to them.

I got the kids out of the water slide and dried them off. I found Erin still running the vacuum cleaner. She cleans thoroughly when she's mad. (All you women may now say "Amen!") I cautiously approached her and asked if we could talk. She followed me to our bedroom, which was a good sign!

Knowing that a soft answer turns away wrath,[7] in a gentle voice, I asked her to help me understand what happened.

"I really needed your help, and you completely ignored my request." Erin explained.

It's important to repeat back what you hear so your spouse can feel understood. (Remember chapter 3 on "reflection"?)

"So you felt ignored," I repeated.

"Yes," Erin responded. "I also felt alone—that cleaning the house was just my responsibility. I would have loved to have been a part of washing the cars, having a water fight, and watching the kids play on the slide, but I can't relax until the house is clean when we have company coming later on. I would have been too preoccupied with the housework to enjoy playing with the kids."

"So you felt alone and left to clean the house on your own." Erin nodded her head in agreement. "It also sounds like you can't relax and play when there's housework looming."

It would have been easy for me to debate if I had really "abandoned" her or to point out that she just needed to learn to relax, but that would have only made us more disconnected. Her feelings are her feelings—they're neither right nor wrong, good nor bad—they are the voice of her heart. I want Erin to know that she matters to me and what she is feeling is important to me, whether it makes sense to me or if I agree with them or not.

But once I heard how she felt, I instantly took responsibility and apologized. "I'm so sorry you felt I wasn't there for you. I'm equally responsible for our home and for managing our children. I was wrong to blow off your request. Will you forgive me?"

"Yes," Erin said and smiled. "Thank you."

"I forget you need to have the house cleaned up before you can relax and play—especially when we have company coming," I explained. "That's so different from me."

Erin then asked me what happened for me. I could tell her heart was open just by the way she asked the question. If she had still been upset, I may not have offered my feelings to her at this moment. I might have said, "Let's talk about me later."

Instead, I explained, "I felt controlled. It felt more like you were demanding help with the housework instead of asking me to help figure out a win/win solution to get the house cleaned. I didn't feel like I had a choice—it was your way, or I'd be in trouble. I didn't feel like you were willing to consider what I wanted or if I had a timeframe for the day's activities and chores. Besides, the kids were already in their swimsuits, and I had promised we would play in the water."

Conflict is inevitable; combat is optional.

Max Lucado, *When God Whispers Your Name*

"It sounds like you felt controlled because I didn't ask you to help decide when to clean the house." Erin replied. "And the kids were ready to play because you promised them."

"Yes." I nodded. "And then when you got frustrated, I felt disrespected by the way you were talking to me."

Erin summed up what she had heard, "You felt disrespected by my words when I became upset."

"Yes," I said. "Thank you."

"You're right," Erin said, "I didn't ask about your expectations for the day—when we would play and when we would clean. I didn't know you had made a promise to the kids. And I was hasty with my words. I'm really sorry, would you forgive me?"

"Absolutely," I responded.

After a big hug, we both went to the kids and apologized for how we acted. We then divided up the remaining housework and we all finished cleaning the house together. Once the chores were done, we all went back outside to the water slide and played until dinner and the arrival of our guests.

Certainly, all our conflicts don't end like a rerun of *Full House*, but we can usually get to a good place once we get our hearts back open and talk things through.

We've come a long way since Hawaii and Hurricane-O.

In the next chapter, we'll discover that honoring your spouse is also a key to maintaining a committed, love-filled marriage.

TRUE LOVE HONORS

Do nothing out of selfish ambition or vain conceit.
Rather, in humility value others above yourselves.
—Philippians 2:3 (NIV, 2011)

I've officiated my fair share of weddings and witnessed some slipups. I've seen groomsmen trip, brides drop bouquets, ring bearers burst into tears, and best men botch toasts. I've even embarrassed myself by pontificating about garden fertilizer while the audience was giggling at the double entendre that everyone caught—except me.

Trust YouTube to turn the "blushable" moments to an even deeper shade of red. The humorous video collections usually involve a fall: party tents, pants, brides, ministers, and cakes all seem to topple, causing spectators to laugh.

But there's one "fall" during a wedding that no one laughs about: a fall from grace. One of those made the news a couple of years ago. Right before making his vow to love, honor, and cherish the woman standing before him, one hapless Chinese groom uttered the name of his first crush . . . and she wasn't his bride!

The affronted woman in white demanded an immediate end to the ceremony and a divorce. (In China, the legal contract is executed before the ceremony.) A news commentator afterward called the groom's error a "defining moment."[1] I paused and thought that the groom's mistake wasn't what set the tone of the relationship. It was the bride's choice to respond in anger. What would have happened if the bride had instead responded with grace, as if she valued the groom more than she valued her pride?

WHAT DEFINES YOUR MARRIAGE?

I think I've already established that I had a lot to learn about love the day I married Erin. Even though I was the son of a nationally renowned marriage expert, a lot of my dad's advice rolled around in my head like pinballs, and not many of them landed in a hole that racked up relationship points with Erin. But I can attest to one thing about being raised by Gary and Norma Smalley that scored a hit in my heart and mind.

While others of you were probably lectured on the merits of "honesty," "discipline," and "politeness," which are certainly lecture-worthy attributes, my home was also steeped in the use of the old-fashioned word *honor*. It's one of the hallmark principles my dad teaches in virtually all his marriage material. More than that, he still *lives* it, showing honor to my mom nearly every opportunity he can. *Honor* is the term that defines my parents' marriage.

The List

This story is part of my family lore, and I share it every chance I get because it shows the power of intentionally choosing to view someone as valuable. It illustrates the principle of honor in action.

In 2008 my family spent the Thanksgiving holiday weekend with my parents in Branson, Missouri. At one point, they got into a huge argument. I couldn't even tell you what it was about, and I'm sure they don't remember either! (See, I told you conflict is inevitable! That's why having short accounts is so important.)

In frustration each stomped off to different parts of the house. Of course, all the women chased after my mother to provide emotional comfort and support. Since I was the only adult male present, I figured I'd better chase after my father. But instead of empathy or emotional support, I reasoned that my dad needed to laugh.

As I trailed my father toward his home office, I suggested what I thought was a good idea. "Hey, Dad," I said with a chuckle, "since you've written, like, fifty marriage books, how about if I pull one off the shelf and read what you should be doing for Mom right now?"

I thought my banter was quite funny.

The door to his office slamming in my face indicated he disagreed with me.

I let him calm down for a few minutes before I knocked on his door.

"Come in," he reluctantly replied.

As I walked into his office, I found my dad sitting behind his computer. I assumed he was online reading the news or looking at the weather. But when I walked up behind him, I saw the screen. The content surprised me.

"What is that?" I asked.

"Well," my dad began, "a number of years ago I started a list of why your mom is so valuable. So when I'm upset with her or when we've had a fight, I've learned that instead of sitting here thinking about how hurt or frustrated I am, I make myself read through this list."

"A number of years ago I started a list of why your mom is so valuable."

The document contained hundreds of words and phrases describing my mom's value. It was amazing.

"When I first start to read through the list, I'm usually still upset," he explained. "I get to the first three or four items and I think, *What was I thinking?* or *This one is no longer valid!* or *I'm definitely going to erase that one.* But the farther down I read, the faster I realize that Norma is an amazing woman."[2]

The Honor Role

Erin and I have come to believe honoring is key for building a strong and safe relationship.

Other marriage experts agree with us (and it's not just my dad). Marital expert and bestselling author Dr. John Gottman identifies honor as perhaps the most important key to a satisfying marriage. Gottman writes that "Without the fundamental belief that your spouse is worthy of honor and respect, where is the basis for any kind of rewarding relationship?"[3]

The Free Dictionary defines *honor* as "to hold in respect; esteem." In practical marriage terms, Erin and I define it as a decision to see another person as a priceless treasure—recognizing his or her incredible worth and value. That wording choice is, in part, taken from the Greek word for honor: *timē*, which means, "what has value in the eyes of the beholder," and "perceived value," and "worth, literally 'price.'"[4]

This isn't something that must be earned by your spouse. It is given, unconditionally, or your spouse's emotional and/or spiritual health will suffer. One Old Testament passage that breaks my heart is about Leah, the unfavored wife of Jacob, who has just had another child, and says, "God has presented me with a precious gift. This time my husband will treat me with honor, because I have borne him six sons" (Genesis 30:20). That's right, *six*. Leah never "earned" the honor she was due from Jacob, even after giving him half the tribes of Israel and a daughter as well.

ERIN'S HONORABLE MENTION

You may be wondering how I could start a why-I-value-Greg list while we were fighting so much in the early years of our marriage. I had to focus on the big things, the parts of his character that had caught my attention in the first place. And even though things were bad some days, I was still able to treasure hunt, to look for the good in our relationship.

1. Greg is my best friend.
2. Greg is a lot of fun to be around.
3. Greg and I share a spiritual connection (even though it was weak early on).
4. Greg has a vision and a goal to help hurting people.
5. I admire Greg for pursuing a PhD.
6. Greg has a vision from God, a calling.

The Value of a Great Spouse

To be fair, Jacob was entrenched in a polygamous culture and tricked into marrying Leah by her father. We don't have those excuses. Proverbs 31:10 says, "An excellent wife, who can find? For her worth is far above jewels" (NASB). I believe a good husband is worth at least as much—a viewpoint which leads into an explanation about the rest of this section. Because the cultural bias of the biblical texts is aimed at men to treat their wife with honor, it may sound as if men are the only ones who need encouragement to treat their spouse properly. However, it may even be more difficult for women to honor and respect their man. This husband-wife tension is described in Genesis 3:16 when God says to the woman Eve: "Your desire will be for your husband, and he will rule over you." Some of the repercussions of the fall (Genesis 2) for women are relationship issues in regard to power, which, more likely than not, need to be resolved on a daily basis.

Of all the things love dares to do, this is the ultimate . . . Though challenged, it keeps moving forward. Though mistreated and rejected, it refuses to give up. Love never fails.

Stephen and Alex Kendrick, *The Love Dare*

I assure you, while the roles of men and women in marriage often present or manifest differently, the responsibility falls on both spouses to love, honor, cherish, and respect the other, reciprocity being the main emphasis. Wise spouses follow the lead and temper of this verse: "Do nothing out of selfish ambition or vain conceit, but in humility consider others better than yourselves" (Philippians 2:3).

ON MY HONOR

While we were dating, I made a big to-do about the importance of honoring Erin, but it took me a while before I knew how to act that out on a daily basis. One of the first things I learned, however, was to never, ever disparage her in public.

Now this was more difficult for me than it should have been because when I get in a crowd, being the center of attention by garnering laughs is my style. Often I use self-deprecating humor and just as often, it works well. (For example, you've now been chuckling at my expense for twenty thousand words or so.)

Once I got married I figured I'd have double the fun because I could now get laughs about Erin too.

At one of our first formal dinners as a couple, I was sitting next to a kind, older couple. I made a joke about Erin's propensity to worry (I can't tell it again because that would be the back door to disparaging her), and I didn't think anything of it. But the kind man next to me did. So when I later asked him how long he'd been married (fifty-six years), I followed up with another question, "What have you learned about marriage in those years?"

He offered some advice, which was really a thinly veiled censure. "I will never talk bad about my wife," he said. "I will never disrespect her. I will never complain about her when I'm in a group of men. I will never make jokes about her. I will always be loyal to her in public."

His words were like a bitter pill, but fortunately I wasn't too proud to take my medicine and swallow it.

I started with the goal of honoring Erin, but I've had to learn how to do it, to change my ways, to listen to her, and to be creative in finding new ways to show her how valuable she is to me.

YOUR SPOUSE IS YOUR
NEAREST NEIGHBOR

Erin and I believe the master plan for building honor in your marriage begins with a straightforward directive from Jesus: "Love your neighbor as yourself" (Matthew 22:39).

In a day when that can refer to everything from building self-esteem with a life coach to coloring your hair, what does it truly mean to "love yourself?"

The answer can be found in the apostle Paul's words to the church at Ephesus regarding marriage:

> So husbands ought also to love their own wives as their
> own bodies. He who loves his own wife loves himself; for
> no one ever hated his own flesh, but nourishes and cher-
> ishes it, just as Christ also does the church, because we
> are members of His body. FOR THIS REASON A MAN SHALL
> LEAVE HIS FATHER AND MOTHER AND SHALL BE JOINED
> TO HIS WIFE, AND THE TWO SHALL BECOME ONE FLESH.
> This mystery is great; but I am speaking with reference
> to Christ and the church. Nevertheless, each individual
> among you also is to love his own wife even as himself,
> and the wife must see to it that she respects her husband.
> (Ephesians 5:25-33, NASB)

Pay particular attention to this portion of the passage: "So husbands ought also to love their own wives as their own bodies. He who loves his own wife loves himself; for no one ever hated his own flesh, but nourishes and cherishes it, just as Christ also does the church."

Since Erin and I have already presented our case for the sacrificial love required in marriage, we'll focus on the day-to-day ways to honor your spouse. In simple practical terms, you "nourish" and "cherish" your own bodies, and you should do that for your marriage partner. Building a solid foundation of honor in your marriage happens when you choose to regularly cherish and nourish each other.

> While I didn't use the word honor in my wedding vows, I used its twin: cherish.

While I didn't use the word *honor* in my wedding vows, I used its twin: *cherish*. For the rest of this chapter, the terms *honor* and *cherish* are interchangeable. (We will explore *nourish* next.)

HONOR IN BIBLICAL ACTION

Remember the Bible character Ruth, the widowed Moabite woman who left her home country and "burned the boats" in order to follow her mother-in-law? The next part of Ruth's story reveals a great act of honor between a man and a woman, one so romantic it gives Jane Austen a run for her money.

Introducing Boaz

I find it charming that the King James Version of the *Holy Bible* refers to Ruth as a "damsel." And Boaz makes an outstanding knight. In Ruth chapter 2, the text says Boaz is a kinsman of Naomi's husband, a close family friend. He is a man with considerable social standing in Bethlehem. While the text doesn't say he's a hunk—tall, dark, and handsome—the Bible tells us he's something even better: worthy.

Boaz is also older than Ruth. He's not a doddering invalid, but neither is he a spring chicken, to use the Southern term. He's still physically fit, as demonstrated by his practice of walking his fields during the heat of day and winnowing grain himself. So I'm estimating his age to be fifty-ish and Ruth's to be mid to late twenties.[5]

Boaz's family has an unusual past: his mother was the one-and-only Rahab-the-harlot-turned-hero, a convert who believed in "the God in heaven above and on the earth below" (Joshua 2:11). But his mother's somewhat unusual background has not held Boaz back.

Respect at First Sight

In the opening of the chapter, Ruth and Naomi need provisions. Ruth's plan to harvest in the fields under the Old Testament provision for widows and the poor[6] takes her to the fields of Boaz, who immediately notices the new girl:

> Boaz asks the field foreman of his harvesters, "Whose young woman is that?"
>
> The foreman replied, "She is the Moabitess who came back from Moab with Naomi. . . . She went into the field and has worked steadily from morning till now, except for a short rest in the shelter."
>
> So Boaz said to Ruth, "My daughter, listen to me.

Don't go and glean in another field and don't go away
from here. Stay here with my servant girls. Watch the
field where the men are harvesting, and follow along
after the girls. I have told the men not to touch you. And
whenever you are thirsty, go and get a drink from the
water jars the men have filled." . . .

"May I continue to find favor in your eyes, my lord,"
she said. "You have given me comfort and have spoken
kindly to your servant—though I do not have the standing of one of your servant girls." (Ruth 2:5-9, 13)

Immediately Boaz begins to cherish Ruth, even by using a
kind tone of voice to comfort her. He provides a safe environment for her. He includes her, as much as is appropriate, within
his household. He offers water, a life-giving essential. But most
of all, he elevates her status from an outsider or scavenger to
that of a servant.

But the cherishing continues! In the next few verses Boaz
speaks kindly to her. He brings her to his lunch table and has
the forethought to save her from social ridicule. The amount
of grain Boaz let Ruth have in one day was beyond her needs,
beyond generous—it was an extravagant gift.[7] And he invited
her back the next day for more!

None of Boaz's actions are for his comfort. Instead he thinks
only of Ruth's well-being, and by extension, Naomi's. In the
end, the couple marries after a midnight rendezvous and some
legal disentanglement.

Do you feel the cherish-vibes yet?

Matthew Henry, a popular Bible scholar, did. He brags on
Boaz:

The conduct of Boaz calls for the highest praise. He attempted not to take advantage of Ruth; he did not disdain her as a poor, destitute stranger, nor suspect her of any ill intentions. He spoke honourably of her as a virtuous woman, made her a promise, and as soon as the morning arrived, sent her away with a present to her mother-in-law.[8]

Boaz and Ruth recognized each other's worthiness almost immediately. As a sunflower turns toward the sun, so Ruth felt safe enough to approach Boaz in humility and vulnerability.

FIVE WAYS TO CHERISH YOUR RELATIONSHIP

Cherishing is a mindset, a mentality, an attitude. It means that you recognize your spouse's incredible value. Can your spouse trust you to treat him or her kindly? Your spouse will feel safe and respected only to the extent that you demonstrate how valuable he or she is. In times of stress, it's easy for us to forget how wonderful our spouse is. Here are some habits to develop so honoring becomes a way of life, even in the trying periods. That behavior will create a place for your marriage to bloom with romance and passion.

#1 Value Your Spouse

The Lord never forgets the value of your spouse. So that you don't forget either, pay careful attention to verses such as these:

- For you were made in [God's] image. (Genesis 1:27)
- You are fearfully and wonderfully made. (Psalm 139:14)
- For you are [God's] treasured possession. (Exodus 19:5)
- You are [a] glorious inheritance. (Ephesians 1:18)

- You are precious and honored in [God's] sight. (Isaiah 43:4)
- A man's greatest treasure is his wife. (Proverbs 18:22) (It's also true to say "A woman's greatest treasure is her husband.")

These verses showcase your spouse in the best light, which is God's perspective. When you treat your spouse as a treasure, then the old adage "beauty is as beauty does" will come into effect. A spouse who believes he or she is part of God's beautiful plan will act in beautiful ways.

#2 Be Thankful and Grateful for Your Spouse
Did you notice that Boaz and Ruth's story shows that he has reason to be thankful and grateful to have her in his life? Boaz hears from his foreman that Ruth works diligently (Ruth 2:7). He notes her worth as a committed daughter-in-law to Naomi and as someone willing to adapt to a new culture and commit to the Lord (Ruth 2:11-13). He knows she is chaste and has a good reputation (Ruth 3:10-11).

When you marry someone, you're in effect promising that you'll be that person's greatest fan. He or she is your lover, your best friend, your lifetime partner to experience the best of times and the worst of times together. It's like Proverbs 5:18 says, "Let your wife be a fountain of blessing for you. Rejoice in your wife all your life" (author's paraphrase). (Or, for the ladies, rejoice in your husband.)

#3 Compliment and Affirm Your Spouse
Many people need to hear words of encouragement every day. Remember Hebrews 3:13: "Encourage one another daily, as

long as it is called Today, so that none of you may be hardened by sin's deceitfulness." It's the second "daily" verse that we explored in "This Thing Called Love."

> *To love someone means to see*
> *him as God intended him.*
>
> Fyodor Dostoevsky, Russian novelist and journalist

A *compliment* is a verbal expression of praise. It's a remark that says something good about someone or something they did. One good biblical example is "Her children arise and call her blessed; her husband also, and he praises her: 'Many women do noble things, but you surpass them all'" (Proverbs 31:28-29).

An *affirmation* is to say something true in a confident way. I affirm Erin when I see the good things about her that she doesn't see—her patience and her tenderness but also her creativity and leadership skills. We use the phrase, "Calling out the value." This sometimes turns into encouragement, which literally means "to make courageous."[9]

THE CALL OF GIDEON

In "Romance Secret #2: True Love Seeks God," I told the story of how my father made the effort to call me out to be my best self as the spiritual leader in my home. I wasn't even aware of the strengths he saw in me. But his view of me changed my view of myself.

Generally, most of us are poor judges of our own God-given

strengths and abilities. So there's a powerful personal impact on our lives when a loved one or trusted friend reaches out to affirm our unique strengths.

Take the story of Gideon, for example. (This is an Old Testament character, not the guy who puts Bibles in hotel rooms.) This Bible hero started out as a reluctant leader during a time when the nation of Israel suffered terrible oppression by its enemies, the Midianites. The Midianites raided communities, burned homes and fields, and killed animals. They left God's people cowering in caves, practically starving.

One day Gideon was at work hiding some of the scarce food when an angelic visitor droped by and asked him to lead God's army.

> The [angel] turned to him and said, "Go . . . save Israel
> from the hand of Midian; do not I send you?"
>
> And [Gideon] said to him, "Please, Lord, how can I
> save Israel? Behold, my clan is the weakest in Manasseh,
> and I am the least in my father's house."
>
> And the LORD said to him, "But I will be with you,
> and you shall strike the Midianites as one man." (Judges
> 6:14-17, ESV)

At first, Gideon felt like a helpless weakling—a nobody—and of little use to his people or to God while the Midianites rained down chaos and devastation. But he was wrong.

God chose Gideon to meet a desperate need, and the angel recast helpless Gideon as a mighty warrior. When he finally saw himself in this new light, Gideon gained the confidence he needed to lead the children of Israel in victory over their enemies.

In the same way, spouses can encourage each other toward

better futures by affirming each other's hidden strengths and true identities in Jesus Christ. Each of us has the power to recast a loved one's self-image, by showing that person his or her true value. When you observe and point out your spouse's unique talents and abilities, you'll see his or her confidence grow in kind.

You have the power to be the best mirror your spouse ever had, changing that reflection to match the vision God intends.

#4 Be Captivated by Your Spouse

"May you ever be captivated by her love" (Proverbs 5:19). Be enchanted, enthralled, fascinated, mesmerized, impressed by your spouse.

This verse shows the positive side of integrity and fidelity, to be so enamored with your spouse that you don't have time or inclination to stray, either physically, visually, or emotionally. If your heart is full of great feelings about your spouse, it's much easier to just say no to lust or to flirtations. Treasure her in your thought life, maintaining purity.

> *Finding other people attractive and looking at them will erode your own view of your spouse.*

The negative side is the warning in Proverbs 5:20: "Do not be captivated by other women" (Or, for the ladies, "other men.") Finding other people attractive and looking at them will erode your own view of your spouse. You will be less satisfied with your spouse, and he or she will feel less special to you.

#5 Be Gracious Toward Your Spouse

Graciousness equals good manners and politeness. Safety is also conveyed by showing respect and consideration. First Peter 3:7

tells husbands to "live with your wives in an understanding way, showing honor to the woman as the weaker vessel, since they are heirs with you of the grace of life, so that your prayers may not be hindered" (ESV). There's no reason women shouldn't also be gracious and understanding. The Greek word *showing* translated here means "to assign, pay as her due."[10] That's what my dad learned how to do even when he was angry.

The Starbucks Lesson

The rise of Starbucks, a 1971 Seattle start-up that is now ubiquitous in American cities, can teach couples the value of cherishing, or creating a "crave" factor. Starbucks is not just about the coffee. It's about cherishing the customer, making a one-of-a-kind experience.

Here's one journalist's take on it:

Starbucks. When you say the name, it automatically conjures up an image: an upscale coffee bar with light wood, glass and chrome. The invigorating and inviting aroma of brewed coffee and the café atmosphere has made Starbucks the best-known specialty coffee roaster and server in the world. . . .

It is that "something special" that defines the Starbucks coffee experience.[11]

When we honor and cherish our spouses they feel comfortable—it's a great feeling, one that they'll want more of. That's the defining difference, the "something special," in your relationship that you're after. Those warm feelings will most likely transfer to intimacy in all areas of your relationship.

En-listing Relationship Tools

The great news is that intentionally creating an inviting atmosphere is possible. You can turn up the relationship thermostat in the same way my dad did—by "en-listing" help.

In the space below, list all of the reasons your spouse is so valuable. For example, you might include a character or personality trait, gender difference, faith pattern, value, moral, parenting skill, spiritual discipline, or even a role he or she takes on that you appreciate.

The following chart might spark some ideas about your spouse's values:

humble	successful
brave	responsible
courageous	helpful
funny	dreamer
loyal	happy
caring	leader
unselfish	gentle
generous	loving
self-confident	neat
respectful	joyful
considerate	cooperative
independent	curious
creative	determined
intelligent	energetic
honest	cheerful
adventurous	thoughtful
hardworking	calm
fun-loving	mannerly

Be sure to keep this list nearby so you can periodically add to it and revise it when you need to remember your spouse's value. Also, don't keep this amazing list to yourself—share it with your spouse. Make it clear that you recognize his or her value. When this happens, not only does your spouse benefit but you are positively influenced as well.

MY LIST ABOUT ERIN

My list about what makes Erin so valuable could go on and on and it does.

1. Highly relational: She loves being with people and relating to people—especially other women.
2. Diligent: She likes to accomplish a lot in each day.
3. Compassionate: She loves to help others when they are hurting—both physically and emotionally. That's why she became a nurse and then a counselor.
4. Passionate: She loves deeply, rejoices greatly, and grieves deeply with a loss.
5. Loyal: She will stand by someone—even when everyone else has walked away.
6. Researcher: She loves to discover new facts and ideas.
7. High achiever: She strives for excellence in everything she does.
8. Networker: She can move into a new city and quickly develop a group of friends.
9. Passionate, deep faith in the Lord: She loves to worship in very traditional ways.
10. Mama bear: If you do something or say something bad about our family or friends, watch out!
11. Laid back: She doesn't get ruffled when things are not organized.
12. Keeps short accounts: You don't have to wonder if she's upset at you or stuffing how she really feels.

13. Adventurous: She loves to try new things.
14. Has integrity: She is devoted to doing the right thing and following the rules.
15. Frugal: She loves a good bargain.
16. Modest: She dresses attractively but not to attract the lustful attentions of men.
17. Sensitive: She loves allowing her heart to feel joy and pain with others.
18. Self-disciplined: She works hard to be healthy by exercising and eating right.

What about your list? What makes your spouse so incredibly valuable? I encourage you to start your list right now. The longer the list the better!

An Honorable Ending

God desires for you to deeply grasp your spouse's value. However, let me be very honest with you: there are times this can be a challenge for anyone in any relationship. Marriage seems to provide many opportunities to love and honor—but to also dishonor. It's all in how we choose to see it.

You can always give without loving, but you can never love without giving.

Amy Carmichael, Christian missionary

Think of honor as a vital fuel that maintains the spark of a loving marriage throughout life. The fire of love might be reduced to embers if neglected or deprived of oxygen. But even a spark of respect or adoration can quickly burst into full flame when it is fueled once again.

Let's hope that's the case for the Chinese bride whose groom said the wrong name during the wedding ceremony. After meeting with a judge, the disgruntled woman agreed to remain married.[12]

Her husband has some honoring to do. At the top of his list should be this: My beloved Zhou—forgiving and gracious from day one.

In the next chapter, we'll discover that nourishing your spouse is a great way to cherish him or her.

TRUE LOVE NOURISHES

Be glad in your GOD. He's giving you a
teacher to train you how to live right—
Teaching, like rain out of heaven, showers
of words to refresh and nourish your soul.
—Joel 2:23, MSG

Currently two of three Americans would be healthier if they lost weight.[1] You might say our country is overnourished.

What would it look like if we were also overnourishing our spouses by meeting their felt needs to the extreme?

"Sex *again*?" you'd hear husbands say to their wives. "Can't right now, dearest. I'm too busy bleaching the grout in the shower. That's way more important."

"Honey," the wives would say, "I'm getting hay fever in the house from all the flowers you've sent this week. You're going to have to limit the bouquets to two a day."

"No, dear," the wives would say, "I don't mind if you go

on a hunting weekend with the guys. Sure, I'll skin the buck if you bring it home. I've seen some venison entrails recipes on Pinterest I want to try."

"Okay, sweetheart," the husbands would say. "I'll turn off the sports channel, and we can go shopping for designer purses. Can't have too many $500 Coach handbags, now can we?"

In the previous chapter, the concepts of cherishing and nourishing were both presented, but Erin and I focused on cherishing. In this chapter, we will unpack the principles of nourishing your spouse—and yes, as the opening examples show, there may be some pandering required. But stay with us, and we'll show you why.

I'll start by reminding you of the key text, Ephesians 5:29: "No one ever hated his own flesh, but *nourishes* and cherishes it, just as Christ also does the church" (NASB, emphasis added). In this passage, Paul reminds the church that people rarely neglect their own bodies, and they are quick to satisfy their own needs for food. In the same way, caring for your spouse's needs should be seen as equally important. You are to labor to nourish your spouse. If you don't, you are essentially starving him or her, and your relationship—and your spouse—will suffer.

I'm not stretching this point at all. The Greek word for nourish is *ektrephó*, which means (1) to grow or to feed, and (2) to bring up to maturity (Christlikeness).[2] In the Bible, it's easy to see the concept of nourishing is analogous to rain; the concepts' meanings are intertwined. Rain is responsible for the growth of food that feeds us.

Jesus explained it this way: "This is what God does. He gives his best—the sun to warm and the rain to nourish—to every-one, regardless: the good and bad, the nice and nasty" (Matthew 5:45, MSG). Here's another example from the Old Testament: "Ask the LORD for rain in the springtime; it is the LORD who makes the storm clouds. He gives showers of rain to men, and plants of the field to everyone" (Zechariah 10:1).[3]

Nourishing your spouse encompasses offering sustenance for his or her physical, emotional, and spiritual well-being. Giv-ing spiritual attention to your spouse is helping him or her pursue kingdom principles. Though the concept is spelled out for a parent and child in the following verse, the idea applies also to marriage: "Fathers! Provoke not your children, but nourish them in the instruction and ad-monition of the Lord" (Ephe-sians 6:4, paraphrased).[4] You're responsible to help your spouse become more like Christ. You're to care about and spur his or her ongoing spiritual, mental, and emotional growth. You're not responsible for the outcome, but you're responsible to nourish this aspect of his or her life.

> *You're responsible to help your spouse become more like Christ.*

A SERVANT'S HEART

Whenever I think of nourishing a spouse through actions, I think of the movie *The Princess Bride*. That cinematic master-piece is part of my life vocabulary. Not only do I chuckle every time I hear the word "inconceivable," but I also worry I'll be tempted to mispronounce "mawedge" and "wuv" while I'm of-ficiating a wedding. And then there's Billy Crystal playing the role of Miracle Max . . .

But I digress.

The true marital value in the movie lies in the opening scenes. Wesley, the farm boy, is trying to win the affection of the farm owner's daughter, Buttercup. The attentive serf does so by being an excellent servant. As he tends to his duties, following Buttercup's orders, his words "as you wish" really mean "I love you."

The origin of the word *servant* is from the mid-fourteenth century, meaning "professed lover, one devoted to the service of a lady."[5] To nourish your spouse, you need to begin with Wesley's "as you wish" attitude, an old-fashioned perspective that seeks to put the needs of your lover before your own.

Jesus' Example

Jesus was the ultimate example of a servant. He served His "bride" by dying for the church. Pastor John Ortberg wrote, "When Jesus came as a servant, he was not *disguising* who God is. He was *revealing* who God is."[6]

How does Jesus want you to reveal God to your spouse? By following His divine example. And what was that example?

Turning water into wine? No. Healing the sick? No. Knocking over tables at the temple courts? No. Fasting? Teaching? Walking on water? No. No. No.

The answer is *foot washing*.

One of Jesus' last acts on earth was to perform the job of a lowly servant and wash the disciples' feet, symbolically making the men clean. Jesus ended the bathing ritual with these words: "Now that I, your Lord and Teacher, have washed your feet, you also should wash one another's feet. *I have set you an example that you should do as I have done for you*" (John 13:14-15, emphasis added).

Following in Jesus' footsteps means to literally and metaphorically "wash your spouse's feet" or serve your spouse with a humble heart. The apostle Paul explained Jesus' mindset when he wrote to the church at Philippi:

> Do nothing out of selfish ambition or vain conceit.
> Rather, in humility value others above yourselves, not
> looking to your own interests but each of you to the
> interests of the others. In your relationships with one
> another, have the same mindset as Christ Jesus: Who,
> being in very nature God, did not consider equality
> with God something to be used to his own advantage;
> rather, he made himself nothing by taking the very
> nature of a servant, being made in human likeness.
> (Philippians 2:3-7, NIV 2011)

So, how does one spouse nourish another with a servant's heart?

If cherishing/honoring is an attitude, then nourishing involves the actions that stem from that attitude. Just as there are some foods that are more nutritious than others, there are actions that can nourish your spouse in powerful ways.

SUPERFOOD #1: JUMBO-SIZE THE SERVING

I'm not going to lie. Nourishing takes effort, and it doesn't always "taste" good. Service, especially at first, can be the boiled collard greens on the marriage menu.

But once you get the hang of service, you'll see satisfying results. You're supposed to dish up large servings of service—think jumbo-size—to nourish your spouse. Jesus said, "Whoever wants to become great among you must be your servant" (Mark 10:43).

I'm convinced this is why the great, proud, privileged Mr. Darcy of *Pride and Prejudice* is still a heartthrob (even among teen girls)[7] two hundred years after Jane Austen penned the classic novel.

We've mentioned Mr. Darcy's propensity for insulting Lizzy before. But I didn't note he's tall and handsome. He's also extravagantly wealthy. But Elizabeth Bennet resists his advances until he is humble and has proved himself a servant. He gives his time, reputation, dignity, and vast amounts of money to serve his ladylove and to keep shame from besmirching the Bennet family name. That's how Darcy wins the hearts of millions of women and captures new fans with every exposure to his noble character.

> *Jumbo acts of service as well as smaller random acts of service catch your spouse's attention.*

Likewise, the character Caleb Holt in *Fireproof* (2008) doesn't win back the affection of his wife, Catherine, until after he sacrifices his savings plan to buy a boat. He forgoes his dream and uses the money for his mother-in-law's electric wheelchair and expensive hospital bed instead. Jumbo acts of service as well as smaller random acts of service catch your spouse's attention.

Why is serving so difficult? Why is 1 John 3:18— "Let's not merely say that we love each other; let us show the truth by our actions" (NLT)—so difficult to live out?

As Erin and I have mentioned before, the cravings of our self-centered natures sometimes override our better selves. It's like craving sugar but knowing you need protein or broccoli. You have to forgo the sugar, and eventually the withdrawal urges go away (or so they tell me!). But here's the crazy thing about service explained by The National Healthy Marriage Institute: "The antidote to selfishness is service. It's difficult to be selfish when you are serving your spouse. Service forces you to put the needs of your spouse in front of your own needs."[8]

SUPERFOOD #2: PREPARE FOR A DISTINCT PALATE

Have you ever been to a nutritionist? If you have, you know that all diets are not equal. Your sex, age, weight, health history, and level and type of exercise all dictate what supplements you need and what foods you should eat—not to mention your personal preferences. There is no one-size-fits-all diet. The same is true for emotionally and spiritually nourishing your spouse. You have to figure out what your spouse needs and what he or she will receive well.

Let me use an example from my experience as a fisherman to explain how you are to study the details of your spouse in order to nourish him or her.

While the weather is good, I like to go fishing for trout. I'll leave early in the morning and arrive at my favorite local fishing river. Every time I fish, I have to study the river and decide where to throw in my line. I have to consider the wind, the shadows, the temperature, and myriad other factors.

New or inexperienced fishermen like my son, Garrison, go back to the same spot every time if they found initial success there. Time and again Garrison will choose the same fishing pool, while I move around the river and often have better success. Learning that you can never fish the same river twice is taught by experience.

One professional angler gave this advice:

> "Don't fish yesterday's fish." Just because you were successful doing something yesterday, or if one tactic worked for a week, or a month, or a year, that was then. You have to figure out the *now*. Tides change, weather changes, fish move. Try to look ahead to the next spot, where you can use the knowledge you gained at your old spot. That's how you repeat success.[9]

GREG'S SCARY NOURISH NEEDS

The first time Greg and I had any significant interaction, I helped his classmates pull a practical joke on him. I now see why I was so attractive to him: Greg loves a good prank. In fact, if you can scare him to near death, he'll forever be in your debt. I've learned to nourish Greg by being sneaky.

One night we were in bed, trying to go to sleep. Suddenly, we heard a noise outside. Greg went to investigate. Alone in bed, I got an idea. While Greg was gone, I shaped the pillows to give the appearance I was still under the covers. Then I hid on the far side of the bed.

When he came back, it was dark and he stumbled around the room. I remained still and quiet at first, and then let out a blood-curdling scream.

Greg's reaction was priceless! He was so scared, his heart rate soared and his adrenaline pumped him up to a new all-time fear peak. To this day he says this about that fright-filled night: "After I changed my shorts and came back to bed, I have never felt so loved."

So it is with marriage. Study your spouse—really listen to him or her, as outlined in "Romance Secret #3." Watch his or her actions carefully. Anticipate. Take notes. Approach finding ways to please him or her as meticulously as you would prepare for a work presentation, a master's thesis, your Fantasy Football league draft, a Christmas party, a great family vacation, or a satisfying hobby. Then you'll be able to provide the right bait with which to nourish him or her. Don't apply the golden rule here!

Superfood #3: Servers, Don't Sit at the Table

Can you imagine the following scenario? You've just ordered a meal at a nice restaurant, and when the server brings you your food, he sits down at your table and takes a hefty bite of your beef Wellington. Then he slurps down your raspberry iced tea and burps. Needless to say, you wouldn't leave a tip; you'd be so angry that you'd report the poor service to the manager.

Erin and I call actions like these *self-service* or *caretaking*—what happens when you "take in the guise of caring." In other words, you are serving to get something in return.

In marriage, caretaking occurs when you are doing good things, but you are the main recipient of the benefits. I've counseled couples who serve each other to keep a spouse from leaving or to get sex later out of obligation. They serve one another to put themselves into the black in the marriage-balance ledger.

Check your motives before you nourish your spouse. Ask yourself, *Why am I serving?* Pause if you are serving to get something. Reevaluate your internal drive until you know you can give unconditionally.

Erin will tell you how I learned that lesson the hard way:

My birthday was approaching, and I could tell Greg was excited. He'd been secretive and overly pleased with himself for a few days.

On the evening of my birthday, he asked me to stay in the bedroom while he prepared a surprise. A little while later, he came to me and asked me to close my eyes. Then he took my hand and led me into the living room.

"Ta-da," he said, joy in his tone. That was my cue to open my eyes.

I will say I was indeed surprised by Greg's gift.

In front of me was an object the size of an overturned refrigerator. Its garish blue and yellow colors were the branding swatches of a vintage Ms. Pac-Man arcade machine.

I tried to gush with gratefulness, but I couldn't. The game was huge. It was ugly. And it was in the center of my living room, my *very small* living room.

Instead of offering my thanks, I blurted, "How much did you pay for this?"

Greg's countenance faltered. "It doesn't matter," he said. "It's the thought that counts."

But in my estimation, he hadn't thought about me at all.

"You don't like it," Greg said.

I shook my head. I was appalled at the prospect of having this freak object in my home. It was moved to the garage, and someone else bought it—for less than a quarter of Greg's purchase price—at our next garage sale.

I bought Erin a gift that would have pleased me. When I saw it for sale, I snapped it right up. It reminded of me of some of our early dates at Red Robin when we'd drop a few quarters into a similar machine. I mean, who wouldn't want to play Ms. Pac-Man all day in the comfort of your own living room?

Apparently, Erin. My gift didn't nourish her; she didn't feel cared for and loved.

Superfood #4: Supplement Your Spouse's Dreams

One way to truly nourish your spouse is to help him or her realize a dream. Erin and I saw the power of God working through our marriage this way several years ago.

One of the promises I'd made to Erin before we got married is that I would be open to adopting a child. Erin is adopted, and she dreamed of following her parents' example and providing a family for an orphan. I was absolutely open to adoption, but I'm sure I would have agreed to just about anything to get her to marry me!

Eventually, Erin's adoption dream became *our* dream, a marriage dream. I could write a book about it (actually Erin is doing that right now), but here's the short, short version.

After having three biological children, we felt our family was still incomplete. At one marriage seminar, we received a sign from God. That's the only way to describe it—we both came away knowing we should adopt a baby girl named Antoinette Rose, after Erin's mother. We'd call her Annie.

We were so excited and couldn't wait to see how God would answer this dream, the desire of our hearts. Erin and I faithfully prayed, but the days turned into weeks, the weeks turned into months, and the months turned into years. Seven years flew by and no Annie.

There is something magical about dreaming together. There is something passionate about working together to unlock those dreams and turn them into reality.

Lysa TerKeurst, *The Power of the Shared Dream*

At one point we began to reevaluate the sign from God. We thought maybe our Annie represented orphans in general and that our job was to financially support ministries involved in orphan care. We began making contacts in the world of international adoptions, and we prayed faithfully for the needs of the organizations and the children in their care.

And then it happened. Through a long chain of bizarre and God-directed circumstances, Erin received an e-mail from an orphanage director that changed our family forever. The woman mentioned the name of a child we'd been praying for. She wrote, "*Annie* is doing great."

That's all it took for God to signal us again. Erin and I aggressively pursued bringing this precious child from China into our family. Today, we've been blessed by our dream baby, Annie, for more than five years.

Nourishing this adoption dream has drawn us closer than perhaps any other single thing in our marriage.

Superfood #5: Refine Your Marriage Menu

If your spouse hates sushi but loves lasagna, don't offer a Japanese menu. Instead, offer Italian. Find the nourishing foods in the language that your spouse prefers. If you don't know, simply ask questions like these: "What do you need?" or "What can I do for you today?" or have your spouse complete the statement: "I feel loved when you . . ."

In order to nourish your spouse's relational desires, you must realize that everyone's are different, based on personal taste. Personalities, interests, gender, backgrounds, and expectations all play into a person's preferences. So before you can begin nourishing your spouse, you have to know what he or she needs from you.

> *Before you can begin nourishing your spouse, you have to know what he or she needs from you.*

Keep your eyes open. Look for daily opportunities to serve, even if you're busy with work or caring for the kids. Sometimes fifteen seconds is all it takes to serve. Can you bring your spouse a cup of coffee in the morning? Wipe down the sink after brushing your teeth? Feed the dog? Make the bed? Do you always ask your spouse if he or she needs anything when you're up? How can you carry one another's burdens as Galatians 6:2 challenges you to do?

Discovering what makes your spouse feel loved is what Dr. Gary Chapman calls finding your spouse's "love language." What makes your spouse feel loved? Chapman outlined five love languages in his bestselling books: words of affirmation, physical touch, acts of service, gifts, and quality time.

The benefit of speaking the right love language is that your spouse feels valued and blessed. And those blessings spread. It shows your spouse that you love him or her, and by extension you show God's love to your loved one.

Superfood #6: Men's Nutritional Needs

Here's a list of nourishment needs that work for me and may work well for other husbands.

- Show me you *like* me as well as love me.
- Be interested in my interests and give me space to participate in them freely.
- Laugh with me.
- Instead of focusing on negatives, highlight what I'm doing right.
- Participate in the things that I like to do even if they're not interesting to you, such as watching football.
- Give me thirty minutes to unwind after I get home from work.
- Compliment me often for what I do that you appreciate.
- Don't concentrate on problems when we go out on a date. Let's have fun!
- Don't overcommit yourself. Leave time for me.
- Give me the benefit of the doubt when I hurt you.
- When you give me advice, don't nag me or belittle me.
- Share your feelings with me at appropriate times and keep it brief—I often feel "flooded" by too many words.
- Share what you appreciate about me in terms of what I "do."
- Remember that I define intimacy as "doing" things together such as having sex, watching a movie, playing Ping-Pong, taking a drive together, or fishing.

- From time to time, you be the one to initiate sex.
- Help me enjoy my day off work, sometimes, without a list of chores.
- Pray with me and for me.
- Don't ask me to be a mind reader!
- Help me learn the best way to show you I love you.[10]

SUPERFOOD #7: WOMEN'S NUTRITIONAL NEEDS

Here's a list of nourishment needs that work for Erin and may work well for other wives.

- Help me to feel safe—protected and shielded from physical, emotional, and spiritual attack.
- Start and end each day by praying together with me.
- Pursue me—show me that I'm your top priority.
- Help me to feel beautiful in your eyes—that you're fascinated and captivated by my beauty and delight in who I am.
- Validate and care deeply about my heart—especially my emotions. Never forget that I won't care what you *know* until I know that you *care*.
- Help around the house with things like folding laundry or unloading the dishwasher without looking for special recognition.
- Encourage me in my friendships and help me spend time with them occasionally.
- Be truly interested in the things I'm passionate about. Support me in those activities.
- Allow me to share my feeling and thoughts without becoming defensive.
- Be the spiritual leader of our family.

- Be a good listener and make eye contact when I am talking. Show me you value what I say.
- When we've been apart for a time and I ask how your day went, don't just say "fine." Please give me details.
- Surprise me with special gifts, a card, or flowers.
- Listen and engage when I want to talk with you.
- Give me time alone to recharge sometimes.
- Continue to court me.
- Hold me and tell me you love me, especially when I'm vulnerable.
- Connect with me during the day. Let me know you're thinking of me.
- Show me affection that isn't just associated with sex.[11]

Tribute to a Superfood Chef

I'd like to tell the story of an amazing woman who inspires many people. Her story is a little somber, but the ending is worth the read.

In 1970, Janine was seventeen when she "had to" marry Herbert "Bertie" Harris and drop out of high school. At first the couple did well financially and emotionally. Bertie had a good job managing the service department at a Chevrolet dealership. Janine stayed home, caring for their baby. They bought a modest home in an East Coast suburb, and they decided to have baby number two right away so the siblings could play together.

About the same time, alcohol also became an addition to their home. Bertie began to drink daily, and as the years flew past, Janine couldn't remember a day when he was happy. Bertie hated his job, the managers, the coworkers, the customers, the hours, the grease. You name it, he'd complain about it and then drink to deal with the anger. He especially didn't like the foreign automobile competition—the Japanese manufacturers able to sell their fuel-efficient cars in the US right in the middle of the gas crisis.

In the early 1980s, Bertie crashed his car into a high school bus carrying a lacrosse team. Everyone on the bus was okay, but Bertie suffered debilitating leg and hip injuries. He had been driving drunk, and the fines, medical bills, job loss, and damages he had to pay put the family in bankruptcy. He also developed diabetes as a result of his drinking, which aggravated the healing process for his leg.

> *Remember, God shaped you for service, not for self-centeredness.*
> Rick Warren, *The Purpose Driven Life*

The only good things left in his life were Janine and the kids. Suddenly everything at the Harris household became all about Bertie. His diet. His health. His addiction. His needs.

Janine despaired that the home she loved went into foreclosure. But when they moved into a small, rental townhome, she made it cozy and welcoming. She also worried about having to work instead of caring for her children full time. Without a high school diploma, Janine's choices of employment were limited. She took the only full-time job that allowed her to pick up the kids from school. And though she liked the work, she didn't earn much as a receptionist at a chiropractor's office.

Despite having a full-time job and the responsibility of raising the kids, Janine was still able to nourish her husband. She made sure he bathed and dressed every morning. She helped him adjust to his strict diet. She patiently cared for him until his health was sound enough for him to get jobs from friends as a handyman. She listened to him complain about the faltering economy, the sluggish sales of American cars, and rising oil prices. She brought him to church events and put him around people who wouldn't condemn him for his poor choices. She did everything she could to foster the relationship between Bertie and their two children. And through God's healing power, Bertie gave up drinking.

> *Janine despaired that the home she loved went into foreclosure.*

Another five years flew by, and when her children began to take courses at the local junior college, Janine enrolled in night courses too, hoping to become a dental hygienist. But that dream got squashed when Bertie had a heart attack and subsequent open-heart surgery. Janine dropped out of school to care for Bertie. A couple of years later, she tried to reenroll, but the criteria for graduation had changed, and her previous courses were no longer accepted.

If you met sixty-two-year-old Janine in the chiropractor's office (where she still works, but as the insurance administrator), you'd admire her trim figure and charming smile. She'd use that smile to beam about her husband. She'd point to his picture on the desk and tell you the next surprise she had in store for him, the new recipe she was going to try, the secret anniversary trip she was planning in Florida. She'd tell you how much she adored Bertie, her husband of forty-five years.

Never once would you hear her say she was too young when

she got married or hear her wish for a divorce. You'd never hear her cry foul that she'd married a drunk, that they'd lost the house, or that she'd had to endure an unchallenging job. She would just get up every morning and give—nourishing Bertie to sustain him emotionally, financially, physically, and spiritually.

The greatest marriages are built on teamwork.
A mutual respect, a healthy dose of admiration,
and a never-ending portion of love and grace.
Fawn Weaver, *Happy Wives Club*

There's many a day I think about people like Janine who commit to nourishing their spouse regardless of tough circumstances. If I didn't know her story, I wouldn't guess what Bertie had put her through. With his wife's ceaseless care and love, he was able to find his way back into the workforce and now is an account executive at a small auto-body repair and paint shop. He's also a small-group leader at church, encouraging young men who are down and out.

Some days marriage is tough for me. Those are the days I think that if Janine can unconditionally nourish Bertie through God's grace, so can I. And so can you.

For date night ideas and a discussion guide, remember to visit *crazylittlethingcalledmarriage.com*. In the next chapter, you'll discover that nourishing your spouse requires a time commitment.

TRUE LOVE NEEDS TIME TO GROW

It is my prayer that your love may abound more and more.
Philippians 1:9, (ESV)

Even a year or more into our marriage, Erin and I weren't mature enough to resolve issues, and it showed. Our mentors, Gary and Carrie Oliver, wisely challenged us to spend a day together doing something fun, to basically go on a date. But there was one boundary: we were not allowed to argue.

The recommendation had a lot of common sense behind it, or horse sense, as they said in the Old West. We loved each other, but we were so busy and so at odds that we couldn't even talk for more than a few minutes without sniping at each other. Having a day of fun sounded great to me, especially since it was going to be an emotionally safe time. I needed to get outdoors in the beautiful Colorado wilderness. Erin needed a break from nursing.

I planned a picnic and a hike to a waterfall, excited to be with Erin. That morning we piled some food and blankets into my old gray Toyota pickup truck and started out on the adventure. It began beautifully; we talked and laughed and sang to songs on the radio. We opened some snack foods to munch on. At some point along the way, however, I made light of an issue that Erin was sensitive about.

Love is a verb, not a noun. It is active.
Love is not just feelings of passion
and romance. It is behavior.

Susan Forward, PhD, therapist, lecturer, and author

She reacted. I criticized her for breaking the Olivers' rule and starting a fight by getting prickly with me. That did not go well. After a few miles, I tried some humor to get her talking again. Well, that tactic was even worse because she completely shut down. At this point, her back was to me and her legs were drawn up as if she was trying to curl up in the fetal position. She was staring out the passenger-side window. Plus, she was eating the snacks and sipping a Diet Coke as if they were for her and her only.

I felt like an idiot, thinking I screwed up the day. It was so awkward that I asked if she wanted to turn around and just go home. I got no answer.

I decided to keep going. If I had to fight with her, I'd rather fight outside in someplace beautiful than fight at home. I turned off the main highway onto a dirt road, heading to the picnic area. The road curved around a massive boulder, and as I steered the truck around the bend, I saw a brown horse standing in the middle of the road. I slammed on the brakes. The horse was not even fazed, but he did back away from the boulder just a bit.

I tried squeezing between him and the boulder, to scoot him away. He stood his ground. I rolled down my window to shout at him, but the horse only moved closer, putting his mangy head into the cab of the truck, his huge, moist nostrils flaring, then closing in the way horses sniff.

Delighted, Erin reached over to pet his ugly nose. I was hating that stupid horse because he could get Erin's attention when I couldn't. I tried to push his head out of the window, but he was too intent on nuzzling around, nibbling on our snack crumbs.

His sniffing paid off because he found something larger than a crumb—a full sized onion-ring crisp. Suddenly his nibbling turned into a bite—a bite right in the worst place possible for a guy . . . my, well, er, ummm, my *lap*. I screamed in pain. That sent the horse running.

At this point, I knew Erin was still mad, but I needed help. I turned to her for compassion—and what did I see? A guilty smirk on her face.

I interpreted the grin as proof she had orchestrated the horse's attack by putting the Funyuns ring on my jeans. We argued about that the rest of the day—neither of us having the horse sense to let it go.

In fact, Erin and I still argue about the Funyun fiasco, although now it's endearing. I joke often about it and ask her if this is the day she's going to confess or if she's going to wait until she's on her deathbed.

If you had asked me that day if I liked spending time with Erin, I would have had a difficult time answering. If you ask couples in different phases and stages of their relationship, you'll get different responses to the question, "How much time should you spend together?"

A man in the initial throes of romance will say, "Every minute." A husband or wife who is absorbed in a career will say, "Two hours every other Saturday." A new mother will answer, "I don't care as long as I get a decent night's sleep first." A quarreling couple will say, "The less time, the better."

"How much time should you spend together?"

If you ask researchers how much time couples need to spend together to make sure love grows, you get more unified responses. I'll summarize here: *as much as you can.* Some specify a weekly amount: fifteen hours was the highest recommendation I found,[1] others recommend around eight hours.[2]

If a person is motivated, he or she can make the time to engage. Consider this disturbing statistic reported by a popular television psychologist:

> The average couple can spend as little as one hour alone together per week; the average couple with kids—sometimes none. The average two people having an affair spend at least 15 hours per week together! Think about that for a moment. Those two people somehow manage to find 15 hours together in spite of all their other commitments, which often include other spouses and children.[3]

If you don't spend time bonding, your marriage will grow cold, and you or your spouse may be tempted to find warmth elsewhere.

THE TIME CONTINUUM

So how much time is really enough time to keep the embers of romance stirring?

Sociologists Jeffrey Dew and W. Bradford Wilcox compiled a report called *The National Marriage Project* in which they determined that a married person who spent "time alone" with his or her spouse "talking, or sharing an activity" on a weekly basis was 3.5 times more likely to say he or she was "very happy" in his or her marriage than a spouse who spent fewer hours with his or her mate.[4]

Talking and doing things together doesn't just happen. You need to be intentional about it. The late marriage expert David Mace, cofounder of the North Carolina-based Association for Couples in Marriage Enrichment, wrote:

> One of the great illusions of our time is that love is self-sustaining. It is not. Love must be fed and nurtured, constantly renewed. That demands ingenuity and consideration, but first and foremost, it demands time.[5]

Now, decades later, Mace's statement is even more relevant. Psychologist and blogger Leslie Becker-Phelps advises to set aside administrative talk and tasks. Find time to discuss heart and dream issues:

> Spend more time together. I don't mean get-more-things-done-together time. Or even air-your-problems time. Partners need to have time when they can each share what naturally bubbles up from deep within—interests, values, or experiences that are expressions of their true

selves. And they need their partners to have the time, focus and interest to really listen. This kind of being together is often lost in the overcrowded shuffling of daily activities. [6]

The Value of Marriage

Valuing marriage makes a marked difference in the quality of commitment. Spending time together says to your spouse, "You matter to me; our marriage matters to me. *We* matter!"

If you act as if you value marriage, the feelings often follow. If you wait till you feel like marriage is important, you may delay planning those special times and they may not happen.

On a similar note, spend money on making those times happen. Hire a cleaning service to free up time for romance and getting emotionally connected. Pay babysitters. Pay for hotels or

---

ERIN'S MEMORABLE WALMART MOMENT

Greg and I decided to be intentional about doing our day-to-day duties together. One of those essential errands is going grocery shopping. I remember one afternoon at Walmart when we split up inside the store. I went over a couple of aisles to find mustard, paper plates, and a few other items. When I returned to the cart, I dumped the groceries in unceremoniously.

"You're not my wife," a man said, smiling. "You can't make me buy this stuff!" He was a stranger giving me a hard time.

Confused, I glanced at the cart. *It wasn't ours.*

Then I heard Greg's laughter. He thought my mistake was hilarious—and so did I. Now we have a great memory because we made an effort to be together.

other lodging. Pay money now so that you can spend time with your spouse or "pay" later in terms of emotional distance and strife. Bottom line: spend money on your marriage.

A friend of mine I'll call Doug recently went through cancer treatment. After Doug finished with chemo, he and his wife sold their home and moved into a townhome, cutting their living square footage in half. He no longer wants to spend time on roof repairs, yard maintenance, or collecting stuff. He has decided they have enough for retirement, so he's spending money on little extras that he never would have before.

> *A man doesn't own his marriage;*
> *he is only the steward of his wife's love.*
> Ed Cole, founder of the Christian Men's Network

Doug let his wife buy a brand-new couch, a former no-no because previously they saved money by purchasing only second-hand furniture. He also accepted the idea of buying organic food at more expensive health food stores.

His wife recently whispered to me, "Greg, that chemo affected my husband's brain. We eat out together sometimes. He wants to visit the kids and doesn't mind paying for the plane tickets. I don't know what happened, but I like it."

I know what happened. After having a wrestling match with cancer, Doug reevaluated what was important and decided that building strong relationships with his wife and children was a priority, something worth spending time and money for today, not a tomorrow that may never come.

LOVED VERSUS LIKED

I would much rather have Erin tell me that she "likes" me than she "loves" me. In my mind, she made a lifelong commitment to love me, meaning she has to love me because it's a decision or an obligation. Her real choice is to like me. Liking me means that she enjoys being around me—that I'm her best friend. Being liked is appealing to me, because it means I'm a priority and that Erin will strive to spend time with me.

This telling scene from *Mrs. Doubtfire*, a hilarious movie on the sobering topic of child custody, shows what can happen if couples don't prioritize and spend meaningful time together. Late actor Robin Williams masterfully portrays the character Daniel Hillard, who dons the costume of an eccentric elderly nanny so he can care for his children after a bitter divorce strips him of his parental rights.

> MIRANDA HILLARD: Daniel was so wonderfully different, and funny! He could always make me laugh.

> DANIEL, AS MRS. DOUBTFIRE: They always say the key to a solid marriage is laughter.

> MIRANDA HILLARD: But after a few years, everything just stopped being funny.

> DANIEL, AS MRS. DOUBTFIRE: Why?

> MIRANDA HILLARD: I was working all the time, and he was always between jobs. I hardly ever got to see the kids,

and on the nights I'd try to get home early to be with them, something would go wrong. The house would be wrecked, and I'd have to clean it up. He never knew, but so many nights I just cried myself to sleep.

DANIEL, AS MRS. DOUBTFIRE: [*crushed*] Really?

MIRANDA HILLARD: The truth is, I didn't like who I was when I was with him. I would turn into this horrible person.[7]

If you let anger and resentment build up, you'll become distant. Keeping those negative feelings under control is exhausting. More often than not, couples are cranky with each other when they don't have enough time together. In marriage, absence does *not* make the heart grow fonder. When you like your spouse and spend time with him or her, you'll also probably like yourself because you'll be at your best. American poet Roy Croft summarized this feeling: "I love you not only for what you are, but for what I am when I am with you."[8]

> *In marriage, absence does not make the heart grow fonder.*

BUSY, BUSY, BUSY

Busyness is what keeps spouses from enjoying time together. It's so hard to find time for your spouse, it seems God didn't make enough time in the day! But He did, and everyone gets twenty-four hours. It's our job to figure out how to manage the onslaught of competing commitments and responsibilities.

Work, kids, household chores, school activities, sports, friends, church, extended family, social activities, and hobbies all conspire to keep you apart from your spouse.

I see it over and over again: Couples don't make spending enough time together a priority, and that might be the primary reason for divorce today. The commitment to spending time together gets bumped down and then off the to-do list. By spending so much time on the job, hobbies, kids, ministry, community-building endeavors, and personal passions, a spouse sends a strong message to his or her mate: *you don't matter*. And when the commitment to the marriage isn't demonstrated in terms of time, look out, trouble is on its way.

There's a fallacy that "one day" couples will have free time, and then they'll work on their marriage. Their intentions are misguided. Life will never slow down, only your bodies will! My dad and mom, who are now in their eighties, are busier than ever, just with different things. If they want to feel close, they have to choose to clear their calendars from other obligations. Some spouses can't even put down the phone, and research indicates that in today's culture bumping your spouse's call to take another is no longer considered impolite.[9]

The first and most important "fight" in your marriage is to resolve conflict. The second is to "fight" for time together. You have to be feisty when you "take on" your calendar. You also need to be stealthy, ever guarding the minutes so the time thief doesn't steal them. Become as dedicated as a special ops agent trained to repel commitments that conflict with a healthy marriage. You also need the physical discipline of a soldier. You must fight fatigue and press yourself to have the energy to spend with your spouse. When children are small, it's difficult to see spending time with them as "the enemy." The danger is that you view time with kids while they're "growing" as priceless, and you make a commitment to them. Meanwhile your spouse is also "growing," but he or she is growing apart from you.

FADING RELATIONSHIPS

Erin and I have managed to work through our issues since the horse-in-the-road episode. (See "Romance Secret #4: True Love Fights for Peace.") But some people don't let go of issues, and they avoid their relationship time together. That behavior is like looking at an old photo taken on a vintage Polaroid camera. Over the years, the colors fade. The defining outlines do too, and if you don't store them properly, you won't be able to identify the people in the photos.

That's what can happen to you as a couple. You can let so many days go without recapturing the romance that over time your relationship will change so much it becomes unrecognizable.

When couples feel lonely in their marriage, they begin to perceive that they have suffered a great loss—their best friend has faded from memory, or worse, died from malnourishment. One writer explains it like this: "Distance in relationships is love's silent killer."[10]

Dr. Dana Fillmore notes:

The reality is, it is virtually impossible to be in love with someone you don't really know and are not connected with; and it is virtually impossible to truly know someone with whom you never spend time; you can certainly "love" them—but be "in love"? No.[11]

You can become so distant, so far apart emotionally, that you no longer desire your spouse, like Miranda Hillard of *Mrs. Doubtfire*. Someone new can come and add infidelity into the picture. Those old family photos will then not only be faded but they may be replaced by new ones with new faces.

CARPE DIEM?

How do you avoid drifting apart from your spouse for lack of time? Here's how I found a solution. It's not pretty, but it works. For many years, I was rigid about my time expectations for our marriage. I wanted entire days if not weeks to spend in leisure with Erin. In certain seasons of our marriage, that was just not possible, and I felt a lot of frustration. While I have never given up on that vision and still believe that longer dates and weekends dedicated to intimacy are needed, they aren't always practical. I now am more flexible, having adjusted my expectations to match reality. And while I can rarely apply *carpe diem*, which means to "seize the day," I can express *carpe quinque*, which means to "seize five" or set aside a few minutes to connect with my spouse.

Seasons of life change, so it's important to grasp snatches of time and redeem them rather than complaining that there's not enough time. Since I've learned that lesson, I have stopped feeling like a failure because we don't get a date night every week—and I even wrote a book about how important they are! I failed to stay connected to Erin emotionally when I was in grad school, but I've now passed through some other stressful periods successfully keeping more or less emotionally and spiritually in tune with her. Those seasons are infant care, starting a new job, moving across the country, being an international speaker, elder care, and losing a parent to cancer.

What if God designed marriage to make us holy more than to make us happy?

Gary Thomas, *Sacred Marriage*

Here's how everyday connection moments look like at the Smalley house: I start my workday routine at 5 a.m. by working out in the basement. Then for a few minutes I watch ESPN with my son, Garrison. While he gets ready for school, I unload the dishwasher. Next I sit on the side of the bed and check in with Erin.

I ask personal questions about her feelings, because that's how she connects with me best. (Remember, I outlined the importance of finding out what nourishes your spouse in "Romance Secret #6: True Love Nourishes.") I might ask, "What's going on with the kids?" or "How are you feeling?" or "What's your day look like?" I don't fix her problems or offer advice. I do commiserate by saying something like, "I hate that for you," or "That's a tough one. I'll be praying for the decisions you have to make."

In the evenings, Erin knows I need to connect by doing something fun. We'll take a quick walk around the block or watch an episode of *Seinfeld*.

Couples have such limited time with each other that recognizing the nourishing emotional superfoods your spouse needs is crucial to making *carpe quinque* work.

You can "anchor" your daily routine to these short but important visits.[12] Creating unique traditions and rituals as a couple should be started from day one. But if you haven't started, then look to today for a new beginning. These rituals are, according to educator Lois Clark, "repeated, coordinated, and significant. Examples of marriage rituals are a cup of tea after the children go to bed, a morning walk before the children get up, or a hug and a kiss upon returning from work."[13]

Another researcher offers this fact for encouragement:

Scientific research says that it is the small, positive moments that matter in keeping relationships satisfied. The day doesn't have to be full of fireworks, but it must have moments of connection—something that can seem difficult when time is scarce. [14]

UNDERSTAND GENDER DIFFERENCES

Just as there are general gender differences in communication styles, so differences also exist between men and women in their expectation of energizing together time.

> *Women are looking for relationship togetherness, a place to express feelings.*

Men prefer to "do things together." Men are looking for the fun, the laughter, the humor, and the sex.

Women are in search of deep emotional connection. Women are looking for relationship togetherness, a place to express feelings.

Meeting the Needs of Men

Have a weekly date night. This is fun time spent away from the house. Couples who devote time specifically to one another at least once a week are markedly more likely to enjoy high-quality relationships and lower divorce rates, compared to couples who do not devote much couple time to one another.[15]

One night a week, go out alone for a minimum of two hours to have fun. The purpose of a "date" is to enjoy each other by asking questions, reminiscing, trying something new. Don't administrate or manage your marriage on a date by talking about the budget, kids, household responsibilities, schedules, or to-do lists. This makes the date feel transactional—like a business meeting instead of a time to connect and have fun.

Also, protect your fun times from conflict. Conflict destroys recreation because it intensifies emotions and people can't relax and enjoy each other. (You saw this in the opening story about the horse biting me!) If this pattern occurs too often, a husband may lose the desire to spend time with his wife because the experience ends up in conflict. Instead of allowing anger and hurt feelings to take over, de-escalate the argument or sensitive discussion by agreeing to talk about the issue at a different time.

The goal of an attentive wife is to plan dates that appeal to a man's desire for activity. Research shows that new activities activate the brain's reward system, creating excitement, exhilaration, and joy.[16] Do things like these:

- hiking
- Putt-Putt golfing
- shopping
- watching a new movie

- bowling
- working out at the YMCA, gym, rec center, or workout club

Women find that these activities inject play and excitement into your marriage. Couples who spend ninety minutes on exciting activities that they did not typically do showed a significantly greater increase in marital satisfaction.[17]

Meeting the Needs of Women

Women need uninterrupted time to feel nourished and loved. So if you only have five minutes, check in with your wife's

---

THE GOOD-BYE GIRLS

Greg and I almost always share a hot drink in the morning before one of us leaves the house. One woman at a marriage conference told us her husband always posts a note on her dressing table before he leaves early in the morning. She wakes up, delighted to have a greeting. Another woman says her husband gives her a gentle kiss before he sneaks out the door. The kiss lingers in her subconscious, and even though she doesn't wake up, she *knows* she's loved. In contrast, a woman I knew a long time ago told me she made the bed over her husband if he slept longer than she did. That's not an everyday moment I'd emulate.

One of my favorite studies to share at marriage conferences is the kiss-good-bye study. More than forty-five years ago, a German researcher studied data that showed men who had wives affectionate enough to kiss their husbands good-bye lived longer, made more money, and were healthier. One other benefit was that their husbands had fewer car crashes. It's an odd statistic, but I'll take the hint and kiss Greg![16]

emotional life. She needs to vent and explain what's in her mind and heart. If she can't release that information, she'll stuff it and get cold and distant or grow hard and angry.

Help her with the evening household duties and turn off your cell phone out of respect when you talk to her. Close the laptop. Turn off the television. Pretend your newspaper, fantasy football league or the stock market report don't exist. Help with the kitchen cleanup and give the kids' baths or supervise their homework; strive to know and be known as outlined in "Romance Secret #3."

Let your wife know she's valued. Compliment her for the ordinary but wonderful things she does—cooking, working, exercising, gardening, driving the kids, volunteering, laundry, or looking nice for you.

The goal of an attentive husband would be show curiosity and interest, to ask her questions that don't have a yes or no answer. For example, ask "How are you feeling emotionally today?"

At the Smalley dinner table we ask the high-low question: What was the highlight of your day and what was the low point? We find that question opens up meaningful conversation about important values and experiences.

Here are some other ideas for activities you can do together:

- Make dinner
- Greet your wife when she returns home—act excited to see her
- Share a cup of coffee in the morning before work
- Thank your wife for something that she did that day
- Compliment your wife on her appearance
- Pray for and with your wife in the morning

- Talk at bedtime but make a rule not to talk about money, work, or the kids
- Do chores together and talk while you work
- Call your wife while you're driving home to hear about her day

Men find these activities keep them updated and current with their wives. These are together times they can look forward to.

Here's one last piece of advice I got from a wise mentor I work with who got the advice from a cancer survivor: "Buy memories, not things." No other use of money will be more satisfying, both now and in the years to come.

Next up, the married couple's guide to great sex: "True Love Embraces."

ROMANCE SECRET #8

TRUE LOVE EMBRACES

Let us go out early to the vineyards and see
whether the vines have budded, whether the grape
blossoms have opened and the pomegranates are
in bloom. There I will give you my love.
Song of Solomon 7:12 (ESV)

I recently heard about a married couple that prays right before they have sex: "Lord, thank You for this gift that we are about to receive." I love the way this prayer puts sex into the right context, but I will never again be able to keep a straight face when someone prays this prayer before eating a meal!

Sex is a wonderful gift given to a married couple by God as a means of experiencing several things:

- Sacred union—a way to experience the deepest, most profound intimacy with our spouse—two becoming one (Genesis 2:24).

- Pleasure—Sex is pleasurable and we are meant to enjoy it. An orgasm creates a rush of endorphins within the brain, which makes us feel good and look forward to repeating the experience.

  Sex and our physical bodies are all God's invention and "very good." One pastor says this is no surprise: "When our first parents consummated their covenant, God was not shocked or horrified, because He created our bodies for sex. The reason that sex is fun, pleasurable, and wonderful is because it is a reflection of the loving goodness of God who created it as a gift for us to steward and enjoy" (Genesis 2:24-25).[1]

- Connection—God uses the phrase "to know" as a way to describe sex in marriage. A couple is never physically closer than the moment they've just had sex.

  Married ten years, wife and mother Rochelle Peachey shares her perspective: "Sex brings a closeness that is beyond words. It relaxes you, puts you in tune with each other, and smoothes over all the everyday trials and tribulations."[2]

  Relationship expert Francine Kaye agrees. "Sex is very much the glue in a marriage. You simply cannot get closer than having sex. It consolidates the bond that keeps people together."[3]

- Procreation—God created us with the intent that a man and woman be equipped to create new life—two making another one. In Genesis 9:7, God told Adam and Eve to "be fruitful and multiply." Our world is continually blessed with new lives and the promise of a future thanks to the gift of sex.

From my own father I learned a valuable lesson about making the most of God's wonderful gift of sex to a married couple. Yes, an uncomfortable lesson—but a valuable one.

Just a few days before my wedding my dad and I were talking, when he suddenly said, "I don't think I've ever talked to you about the key to great sex."

I remember thinking, *And I know why. It's going to include my mother and I don't want to hear it!*

"The key to being a great lover," my dad began . . .

Noooooo!

"I don't ever think about my needs getting met. Do you know what that means?

Yes . . . please stop talking!

"I don't think about me—orgasming."

Dad! No. You're ruining it. Now I'm not even going to be able to have sex because I'm listening to you.

"It's not about you," Dad continued. "You have to put your wife first. It's about being 100 percent focused on her needs—caring about her, pleasuring her. That's what I think about with your mom."

"You've got to stop," I said. "I can't even hear what you're saying because you keep talking about Mom!"

Awkward? Seriously. But I do love that advice because it's about serving your wife.

BE SERVANT-MINDED

God-honoring and marriage-honoring sex is self-giving love. Sex is not a selfish act—a conquest of personal fulfillment. Righteous sex is about self-sacrifice not self-gratification.

A word to husbands: earn the right to enter her body.

A common complaint from husbands: "My wife isn't interested in sex." It's easy to blame this lack of desire on her busy schedule, the endless household responsibilities, the kids, her job, the errands, and so on. Certainly stress and exhaustion negatively impact your wife's libido, but you have no control over the rigors of managing a family. The solution isn't for your wife to ignore her exhaustion and "just do it"—that's not your place to demand.

> *They slipped briskly into an intimacy*
> *from which they never recovered.*
>
> F. Scott Fitzgerald, novelist

Rather, focus on something that you have control over. YOU. Husbands, instead of complaining that your wife isn't interested in sex, you need to earn your way into the marriage bed! I say that this is how God designed our sexual relationship to work.

Look at how are bodies were made for sex. The way a man's body was created implies "initiation" and taking the lead. By God's perfect design, physiologically, before sex is even possible, the man must initiate an erection. The word "erect" means to create, initiate, establish, or build something. Husbands, in the same way that it's our job to become erect before entering our wife sexually, it's our job to first gain access to her heart. Before entering the marriage bed, we need permission and our wife's blessing.

Men like a good quest. Unfortunately, too many men get

their adventure from video games and their romance from porn. Wives, allow your man to court and woo you! Help him to enjoy the adventure of captivating you.

I think one main reason a wife loses her desire for sex is that her husband becomes complacent and stops trying to earn his way into the marriage bed. "What?" you might be thinking, "I thought the apostle Paul said, 'The wife gives authority over her body to her husband, and the husband gives authority over his body to his wife. Do not deprive each other of sexual relations, unless you both agree to refrain from sexual intimacy for a limited time so you can give yourselves more completely to prayer. Afterward, you should come together again so that Satan won't be able to tempt you because of your lack of self-control' (1 Corinthians 7:4-5, NLT). I shouldn't have to 'earn' anything; it's her responsibility to respond. Her body is mine."

Wrong! Although you shouldn't withhold sex from your spouse, you can't adopt an attitude that your wife's body is yours, so you don't need to do anything to woo her. Instead, consider Dr. Mohler's take on the man's responsibility:

Consider the fact that a woman has every right to expect that her husband will earn access to the marriage bed . . . Therefore, when I say that a husband must regularly "earn" privileged access to the marital bed, I mean that a husband owes his wife the confidence, affection, and emotional support that would lead her to freely give herself to her husband in the act of sex.[4]

How does a husband earn his way into the marriage bed?

If you want your wife to be more interested in sex, become "interesting." If she seems indifferent, unresponsive or

uninterested to your sexual advances then become attractive—
allure her and catch her eye. The only time in the Bible that
God acts in the role of a husband is when He is trying to win
back His unfaithful bride—the children of Israel. Hosea 2:14
says, "Therefore I am now going to allure her; I will lead her
into the desert and speak tenderly to her." This is significant.
God the husband isn't saying that His wife "should" respond to
Him simply because it's her duty. Instead, He takes the initiative and pursues His wife. He starts His quest to win her back
by "alluring" her. He is trying to catch her eye—to captivate
her. How does He attract her attention?
He goes after her heart.

> If you want
> your wife to be
> more interested
> in sex, become
> "interesting."

Author and counselor Donald Paglia explains that you might want to
try courting your own spouse: "Part of
what makes a relationship romantic is
the excitement that comes with discover-
ing a new person and noticing that that person cares about you.
Of course, this doesn't mean marrying a new person but rather,
courting your spouse as though you are still bent on winning his
or her love. Basically, it means retooling those very things that
were a part of your earlier relationship but without the threat
of rejection or loss."[5]

"I will lead her into the desert" means that He is taking her
back to the place where their love story began. God is trying
to get His bride away from all of the distractions and refocused
on when they fell in love. Men are great at "wooing" women
before marriage. What did you do to "win" your bride's hand
in marriage?

Be a man worthy of her body. If you want "respect," then be

respectful. Provide for her financial needs, in whatever way possible. Protect her from all dangers—both foreign and domestic. Keep up your physical appearance and have good personal hygiene. Have high moral character. Be faithful.

Be tender. To captivate His wife, God the husband speaks to her tenderly. Tenderness is an aphrodisiac to a woman. This is why a husband is reminded to be tender several times in the Bible: "Husbands, love your wives and do not be harsh with them" (Colossians 3:19) and "Husbands, in the same way be considerate as you live with your wives, and treat them with respect as the weaker partner and as heirs with you of the gracious gift of life, so that nothing will hinder your prayers" (1 Peter 3:7).

> *The key to relationship is not finding the right person. It's becoming the right person.*
> Andy Stanley, pastor and author

Connect emotionally with your wife. Men are quickly turned on and aroused sexually, but women need more time to be ready for that physical connection. They need to feel safe and valued. So create that safety. Invest yourself in a marriage that feels like the safest place on earth to the woman you love.

As mentioned earlier in this chapter, the Old Testament term for sexual intercourse is "to know." (Readers of the King James Version sometimes find it confusing that "Cain knew his wife," or "Adam knew his wife." It might seem obvious that they knew their wives!) Though the language has changed, it's still true today that the intimacy required for a fulfilling sexual connection is based on completely *knowing* your wife and putting her needs above your own.

A word to women: be ready to receive your husband.
This section is from Erin . . .

Ladies, if the husband's body was made to initiate, your body was made to open and receive your husband. By God's perfect design, physiologically, a man's erect penis is received by the open wife. In the same way that you can't control whether or not your husband "initiates," you need to focus on what you can control. YOU. It is up to you to be open and able to receive your husband. To receive means to "accept" or "welcome." Just as you want to create a welcoming spirit in your home, you should also want to have a welcoming spirit to bless your husband.

> ### *When the grass looks greener on the other side, it's time to water your own yard.*
> Jimmy Evans, author and host of *Marriage Today*

Pursue personal availability (get yourself ready for sex). We women are responsible to prepare our "whole person" for sex—to be open. This means we can joyfully serve our husband sexually by nourishing the "whole person" (heart, spirit, mind, body). Let's look at each of these elements in detail.

First, consider how you can prepare your *heart* for sex.

Some women complain: "My husband isn't romantic—all he ever thinks about is sex." I know you care about romance;

that's why so many female readers are drawn to romance novels. If you really want romance, then think about how you can romance your husband. But you have to romance him like a guy wants to be romanced, not like you do. Romance has elements of both a relationship and a love affair. Have you considered having a love affair with your husband?

Just as a man is like a microwave oven sexually, a woman is like a microwave oven relationally. Women can quickly go to deep levels emotionally. But men are like Crock-pots relationally—they are slow to warm up to an emotional connection.

> You might try creating a physical connection first and let the emotional connection follow.

So you might try creating a physical connection first and let the emotional connection follow quickly along behind.

Next, focus on preparing your *soul* for sex.

Praying together, talking about what God is teaching you, embracing the beauty of God's creation, worshipping together—all of these involve what we call "spiritual intercourse." When you connect with your husband about spiritual matters, you are joining together on a very intimate level.

And what does it mean to prepare your *mind* for sex?

It starts with having the right perspective. Some women, even Christian wives, misunderstand their husbands' sexual drive. They see it as a never-ending demand or as something distasteful. It's important for a wife to understand about how God wired her man for intimacy.

Realize that sex "is" intimacy to a man. Though most women need to have an emotional connection in order to have sex, most men can separate the sex act from a relationship. For men, emotional connection flows from physical intimacy. Sex is a man's way of showing his wife how much he loves her.

It can be difficult for a woman to understand a man's sex drive. You may realize that your sex drive is less than his, but too often women completely underestimate how important sex is to their husband. Sex is a legitimate physical need for a man, involving a physiological drive and a need to "release" in a way that isn't typical for a woman.

Men get "turned on" very quickly. Although we women generally get aroused gradually and need to warm up to the idea of sex, men don't require much foreplay, or even forethought, to be ready for sex.

Don't take it personally when your husband doesn't initiate sex. A husband's sex drive can be affected by issues such as unresolved anger, conflict, stress, work problems, pornography, substance abuse, or physical issues including erectile dysfunction and changes in testosterone levels.

Help your husband battle against sexual temptation. Realize that God brought you into his life as a "helpmate." You help your man guard against temptation when he is regularly connected to you sexually. Author Julie Slattery says, "Your husband depends on you to be his partner in his battle against sexual temptation. Although you aren't responsible for his actions, you are a component in his victory. You're the only woman in the world whom your husband can look at sexually without compromising his integrity!"[6]

> *Help your husband battle against sexual temptation.*

Last but not least, consider how you might prepare your *body* for sex.

While physical concerns are often the biggest barrier to a fulfilling sex life, don't passively accept exhaustion, emptiness, fatigue and stress. Become aware of what might be keeping you from receiving your husband sexually. A few possibilities include:

- Stress
- Lack of sleep
- Marital conflict or other relationship problems
- Fear of intimacy
- Hormonal problems
- Wrestling with memories of sexual abuse or sexual trauma
- Depression or anxiety
- Decreased sex drive from the use of birth control
- Certain medicines for depression, blood pressure, and diabetes, which can cause sexual problems
- Guilt over past intimate relationships
- Negative feelings about your own body
- Worries about getting pregnant
- Physical issues such as pain from an injury, diabetes or arthritis
- Experiencing a sexual problem such as difficulty with arousal or orgasm, or pain during intercourse
- Physical changes related to menopause

BECOME A STUDENT OF YOUR SPOUSE

When you do take initiative in improving your sex life, the first thing you need to do is become a student of your spouse. It took me (Greg) ten years of school to become a psychologist. Throughout that time, I was exposed to a fair amount of information on human sexuality. Needless to say, I felt more equipped than the average wife to understand a husband's needs. Boy, did I overestimate my sex education!

Regardless of your background, you have a lot to learn about your spouse's sexuality. In fact, much of what you assume may actually be wrong. If you want a deeply satisfying sex life, you must go back to being a student. Study and observe the ways God made men and women different sexually, and how creating genuine intimacy requires vulnerability, effort, and creativity.

Talk About Sex

As a married couple, we need to feel safe to discuss our sexual relationship together—to talk honestly and openly about our own sexual likes and dislikes.

Complacency can be the kiss of death to many relationships. Making the time and effort to have sex is critical, even if you don't feel in the mood.

Add in Excitement and Passion

Excitement and passion within don't come from experimenting with new positions or techniques. This is what the world wants you to believe. True romance requires curiosity says one expert:

> Within marriage, couples need to cultivate a healthy balance of both certainty and excitement. But therein lies the basic problem: Love seeks closeness while desire needs distance. Too much distance, however, might cause a lack of connection, while too much sameness destroys the attraction of two unique individuals. This is the essential paradox of intimacy and sex.[7]

ERIN ON SEX COMMUNICATION

Yes, sex is complicated. And our situations and needs as individuals are very different. Some women feel guilty when they reject their husbands' efforts at intimacy, while others may blame themselves if their husbands' seem uninterested in sex.

When a woman hears that she should be rested and ready for sex, or initiate it more often, it can feel as if only the husband matters and the wife is just there for his enjoyment. Or after some years, the effort needed to keep sex interesting might not feel worthwhile anymore. A few women may even wish the whole sexual part of the marriage relationship would simply disappear!

As a woman, I want to embrace the gift of a sexual relationship that God has designed. I know how important it is to build and recharge the connection I have with my husband. And I want to keep it a priority in my busy life. But that all can be easier said than done.

Bottom line, a vibrant sexual relationship requires excellent communication. That's the key. I encourage you to pour your time and energy into talking with your husband about your concerns, desires, hopes, fears—well beyond the subject of your likes and dislikes. It is a privilege to share our deep feelings and tackle intimate issues with our husbands. When we run from the conversation, or bury our feelings, we only feel more distant and isolated in marriage.

It helps keep me on track to remember that sex is one of the ways we can serve each other in marriage. The choice to serve is one I get to make. And that act of service can be reluctant or joyful. But when my whole self is on board—mind, body, soul and heart—then I am better able to respond to Greg in love, no matter what else is clamoring for my energy and attention.[8]

So don't fall into a routine, one that can lead to boredom with each other. Seek out ways to keep your relationship fresh and alive. Intimacy depends on familiarity as well as mystery and surprise. Be creative in the ways you reach out to each other, and enjoy your love and sexual relationship as the gift that God intended.

A PROBLEM IN THE BEDROOM?

What can a couple do when they are having problems with sexual intimacy?

It's vital that they look for solutions and not ignore sexual issues in the marriage or wish them away. An excellent resource for couples struggling in this area is Dr. Kevin Leman's book, *Sheet Music*. In it he urges couples to confront the problem:

> Whatever the cause behind your own lack of sexual desire, please, for the sake of your marriage, deal with it! It's just not healthy for a marriage for either partner to show a consistent and persistent lack of sexual desire. It's only a matter of time until the spouse takes this lack of desire personally. To be fair, it's only natural to do so. . . .
>
> By all means, get aggressive in your desire to become well. Go to a good counselor. Deal with the issues that are holding you back. Don't accept the status quo if your disinterest is causing disharmony and frustration in your marriage.
>
> You might keep telling yourself, "I'll deal with it— someday." But eventually, your spouse may say, "Enough is enough!" I've seen too many marriages destroyed by lack of sexual desire on the part of one spouse or the other.[9]

So do whatever it takes. Get counseling. Schedule a checkup. Seek medical help if necessary. Don't give up looking for an answer and for improvement.

In the meantime, be sure to practice patience, grant forgiveness, and keep the relationship healthy even when the physical side is lacking.

Don't Wait for Help

Because a couple's sexual relationship has such a profound impact on their emotional relationship, a problem left alone can grow to extremes. In one case, a couple went through years of heartbreak and pain before they came to me for help.

The shy young man and woman sat in my office, there for the first time. They explained that they were virgins when they got married. Neither knew much about sex, and the bride had not followed up on a premarital counselor's suggestion to get a physical examination before the wedding. So it came as a complete shock to both of them on their honeymoon night when they were unable to have intercourse (a problem caused by the bride's undiagnosed condition called vaginismus).

The night went downhill rapidly. He blamed her, suggesting she had done something wrong and was being punished by God. Of course, that caused her to shut down emotionally. And, not surprisingly, their next attempt at intercourse also failed.

Unable to consummate the marriage, the groom left in anger. The honeymoon was ruined, and the new marriage was off to a poor start, to say the least. "Four years have gone by," the husband told me, "and we've never had sex."

Four years! The damage that was done emotionally and relationally during all that time took much effort to repair. Of course, the wife was immediately sent for a diagnosis and medical care, but the real work required this couple to establish emotional openness again.

*I've seen you at your worst
and I still think you're the best*
Tony DiLorenzo, *One Extraordinary Marriage*

I'll never forget the day the pair came back into my office, faces beaming, both giddy as a couple of teenagers. "You had sex, didn't you?" It was an easy guess.

Finally this couple was restored to the marriage they had wanted all those years ago.

If you have a physical issue, seek out professional, medical help. There are many options that might make a world of difference and enable physical closeness in your marriage to spark intimacy and joy.

And remember, the need for a fulfilling sex life can be as strong on a wife's part as on her husband's. Nearly a century ago, a woman known as "Frau S" determined not to let anything come between her and her husband. Though her man was away from home fighting the Great War, she wrote this letter to his commanding officer.

2 January 1917

Dear Leader of the Company!
I, the signer below, have a request to make of you. Although my husband has only been in the field for four

months, I would like to ask you to grant him a leave of absence, namely, because of our sexual relationship.

I would like to have my husband just once for the satisfaction of my natural desires. I just can't live like this any more. I can't stand it. It is, of course, impossible for me to be satisfied in other ways, firstly, because of all the children and secondly, because I do not want to betray my husband. So I would like to ask you very kindly to grant my request. I will then be able to carry on until we are victorious.

With all reverence,
Frau S [10]

If Frau S was willing to go to such lengths to unite with her husband in their marriage bed, shouldn't you too fight your way through any barriers to enjoying sexual intimacy together?

I think our dear war friend would have appreciated some of Erin's and my favorite advice from John and Stasi Eldredge in their book *Love & War*: "You need to do it. Often. In a way you both enjoy it. Immensely."[11]

Make love and not war is a great thought—don't forget it. Next up is a chapter on how to negotiate the chore wars, "Romance Secret #9: True Love Serves."

TRUE LOVE
SERVES

*Finally, all of you, have unity of mind, sympathy,
brotherly love, a tender heart, and a humble mind.*

1 Peter 3:8, ESV

Picture this: A married couple returns from vacation, exhausted. Their oversized suitcase gets plopped down on the landing of the living room stairs—where it sits in plain sight. And sits. For three weeks.

Ray, the husband, thinks it's his wife's job to move it upstairs. After all, it's full of dirty clothes, and laundry is her responsibility. So he "ignores" it.

Wife Deb also pretends to ignore the baggage. Until she says angrily: "I have to do everything around this house. I'm the one that has to do the laundry. Why should I be the one to drag that thing upstairs? Isn't the *man* supposed to carry stuff?"

The multi-week, passive-aggressive battle isn't lost on a frequent visitor, Ray's dad. Frank tells his son, "Hey, listen to me. This is not about a suitcase. This is about who wears the pants in the family."

Finally, Ray and Deb realize they are behaving like stubborn children. Until another tug-of-war breaks out—a mad scramble as each tries to "win" by being first to haul the suitcase upstairs.

If you're a fan of the classic sitcom, you'll recognize this story as the fourth highest-rated episode of TV's *Everybody Loves Raymond.*[1] What made it one of the top episodes out of hundreds? It was a fan favorite because married couples could identify with its universal themes: the split over "who does what?" and the power struggles that often crop up over seemingly minor disagreements. It's funny because it's true.

Is it wrong for spouses to disagree? No. Honest disagreement can be healthy for a relationship—we saw that in "Romance Secret #4: True Love Fights for Peace."

But when you consistently feel as if you are in a never-ending battle over household responsibilities and roles, your relationship begins to feel adversarial. If you and your spouse constantly go from being teammates to opponents, your marriage will quickly start to feel unsafe.

The unhealthy result of disunity in a marriage is an unresolved power struggle. Almost every couple has encountered this, often early in the marriage. For instance, a typical power struggle occurs when couples get into a relational tug-of-war over who will do what in order to manage their home—inside and out. The result can fracture the bond that holds a couple together.

This is exactly what Jesus meant when He said, "Any kingdom divided against itself will be ruined, and a house divided against itself will fall" (Luke 11:17). Unhealthy power struggles destroy relationships because the outcome is guaranteed. A marriage divided will fall!

CHORE WARS DEFINED

There's a wide range of subjects a couple can choose to argue about: money, household chores, children, sex, work, leisure time, in-laws, and more. Yet research reveals that married couples are surprisingly similar when it comes to issues that lead to harmony or discord on the home front.

A whopping 70 percent of adults say "sharing household chores is 'very important' or 'rather important' to marital success." For this topic, little variety of opinion exists between genders, people in different age groups, or single versus married individuals. People are amazingly unified in this observation.[2]

Is that true in your own marriage? If so, you are not alone.

The Bad News that You Probably Know

Many husbands and wives perceive the division of housework as unfair and end up in conflict. They spend an enormous amount of time arguing over who's going to care for the children, cook meals, do yard work, clean the house, take out the trash, fold laundry, pay bills, walk the dog, clean the dishes, grocery shop and run the kids from activity to activity.

Feelings of resentment—of being taken advantage of and unappreciated—snag the fabric of the marriage.

The Good News that You Probably Don't Know

The good news is that according to a Pew Research Poll, sharing household chores ranks as the third highest issue associated with a *successful* marriage—behind only faithfulness and good sex.[3] This means if you can learn to share chores, your marriage will have one of the hallmarks of unity.

There are more benefits of being able to negotiate peace in the chore wars than merely having a clean home. Dr. John Gottman notes that the happiest, and most sexually satisfying relationships, are those where husbands participate equally in childcare and household chores.[4]

As we focus on specific problems associated with sharing household responsibilities, keep in mind these insightful words from Frank Barone: "It's not about the suitcase."

MOVE PAST WINNING

The real issues go much deeper than who empties the trash or mows the lawn. And the resolution shouldn't be about "winning" either. What's important is the way you work through common, day-to-day concerns. The right approach can establish a solid foundation for working through the bigger obstacles that will inevitably come up in your life journey together.

Let's consider four major challenges that confront couples trying to break out of the chore wars. Each challenge is based on a very human, flawed point of view. You won't have to look too hard to find yourself and your spouse in some of these all-too-common conflicts.

Challenge #1: "It's not fair!"

It's true that distribution or division of chores and other household responsibilities is often unequal and unfair. Even when couples try to share the load evenly, it doesn't always work out that way in real life.

Surveys and studies point out that even though many women work outside the home, they still tend to do most of the household chores. Men typically do about 9.6 hours of housework each week; women typically do about 18.1 hours. Where childcare is concerned, men average about seven hours a week, while women put in about fourteen hours caring for the kids.[5]

This common inequity can leave a spouse feeling alone or taken for granted. Have you ever felt or said one of the following? Or heard it from your spouse?

"I have to do everything."

"You're not pulling your weight."

"You want me to do more work when you've been having fun all day."

"You don't value what I do for our family."

"At least you're not stuck at home with the kids all day."

The chore wars can develop into a never-ending debate about which spouse does more. I hate to admit it, but Erin and I have had nasty arguments about this. For a time we almost weren't able to talk about it rationally.

Sometimes it stems from a communication problem, when each spouse is unaware of what the other does during the course of a day, or a week. I mentioned in "Romance Secret #3: True Love Seeks to Know and Be Known," that Erin would call me whenever I was on the road. At that time in our marriage, she felt overly burdened by the housework because I wasn't there to help. I don't think I fully appreciated how difficult being a stay-at-home parent is and how feelings of isolation can build up.

Often spouses wear blinders, fully understanding only their own jobs and roles in the household. I know exactly how challenging my job is, for example, even if Erin doesn't grasp that.

She's a better at administration than I am, for example, and what may seem easy to her are tasks that just about floor me every day.

> *Often spouses wear blinders, fully understanding only their own jobs and roles in the household.*

As a result of making assumptions and failing to communicate openly, one or both spouses can end up feeling invalidated, devalued, minimized, or marginalized.

Challenge #2: "It's not good enough!"

The way an individual is "wired" or designed by God can contribute to widely different expectations within a household. Some individual preferences may not make sense to a spouse with an alternate set of priorities.

While some credit our differences to gender-related characteristics (women tend to be nesters and nurturers; men are providers and protectors), it's true that differences between individuals are broader than the differences within groups. So even if a wife wonders if the men in her family can even *see* the dust that drives her crazy, it could just as easily be the husband who despises dust and craves order in the house.

Some expectations are set based on your family of origin. Maybe Mom was a perfectionist; Dad only did masculine chores. Or a spouse might rebel against an overly rigid home life and choose to let household duties slide intentionally.

Some spouses do more housework because they actually prefer cleaner or tidier homes. They may want the laundry sorted in a specific way or have an unvaried routine for cleaning the kitchen floors and counters. Others wait until company is coming, then clean in a frenzy of action. And some people just enjoy a house with that "lived in" look.

I admit to being a true caveman. Recently we were having company over, and Erin wanted help cleaning the refrigerator. To her, it was a bastion of ooze and bacteria. I looked in and thought, *No maggots. Looks good to me.*

> **When you love you wish to do things for. You wish to sacrifice for. You wish to serve.**
> Ernest Hemingway, *A Farewell to Arms*

If you're like us, take a personal inventory and be aware of your own preferences about cleanliness. I hate changing sheets and making the bed, for example, but I'm fine with washing the cars or unloading the dishwasher.

In general, women have lower tolerances for both dirt and disorder, so they might expect certain household chores to be done more frequently than the men in their lives. This often means they get stuck doing much more than a fair share of such chores.

The problem arises when there's a major disagreement involving preferences and priorities. Even if I don't want to clean (that's my personal preference) but Erin does want to clean, I have to jump in or pay the consequences.

In the chore wars, the "cleaner" seems to win most often. Or you end up in a standoff, like Ray and Deb, who left their suitcase on the stair landing for three weeks. That is, until Ray was leaving town and stuffed a piece of stinky cheese inside the bag before he left. Seriously, these battles can get ugly—and smelly!

Is there a form of compromise? Do less? Do more? When both husband and wife work outside the home (and in 2014, 47.7 percent of married couples were both employed),[6] there just isn't enough time to get everything done. So choosing what gets priority comes down to preferences and individual desires.

Each spouse has an idea about what needs get done at the bare minimum. (Typically I'll choose downtime over cleaning most any day.) So these household chore preferences will create conflict when spouses can't agree on the basics.

Challenge #3: "It's not my job!"

Erin and I have been married more than twenty-four years, and dividing up household chores is certainly an issue we've consistently faced. Something happened not too long ago, however, that has completely changed my perspective about this reoccurring frustration. I have told this story once or twice, because it was a turning point in the chore wars for us.

One evening after work, as I walked into the kitchen, I could hear what sounded like pure chaos. Erin was busy making dinner, two of our four children were engaged in an argument, the TV was blaring, and someone's homework was scattered over the counter and onto the floor.

Hearing the metaphorical ticking time bomb, I uttered four little words that changed my life, "How can I help?"

At first glance, this phrase sounds positive, right?

"How can I help?" In other words, "I can see things are out of control and I want to assist in some way because I love you."

The sad part about it is, when most people promise for better or for worse, they really only mean for the better.

Ken Bevel as Lt. Michael Simmons in *Fireproof*

I thought this offer would emphasize my "loving husband" nature. Certainly my heart was in the right place, but I quickly realized that I was unknowingly creating a huge rift in my marriage. The evidence was how Erin responded to my gracious offer: "You're a big boy. Look around. See what needs to be done. Jump in and do it."

To be honest, at first I felt hurt. But then I quickly moved to righteous indignation: *The nerve,* I thought. *I can't believe she just snapped at me after I offered to lend a hand.*

And that's when the epiphany happened. As I stood there sulking, I realized that my offer to "help," in many ways, implied that Erin was solely responsible for the work that needed to be done around our home. And I was offering her my help as an assistant and not as co-owner.

I appreciate Jim Thornton's funny take, in his book, *Chore Wars,* on what a wife really hears when her husband offers to help:

We both know these chores are your ultimate responsibility, dear, but if you spell out exactly what you want me to do, I will begrudgingly help you with our work. And, by the way, you better show me some appreciation for my help. And if you want me to help again, you will have to remind me each and every single occasion this obnoxious task comes up.[7]

That night as Erin and I talked, I sought forgiveness for any time that I'd unintentionally implied that she was solely responsible for the housework and that I was just her "helper." I made sure that she knew that we were teammates and that I was also 100 percent responsible for the care and maintenance of our home and children.[8] Sure, I could have debated how I contribute by working full-time outside the home, but that would have only driven us down the same old dead-end we'd run into many times before. Because the issue isn't about work *inside* the home or work *outside* the home. It's about equal ownership of all the tasks and responsibilities that are part of family life, no matter who ends up meeting an immediate need.

So don't fall into the trap. Asking for help can give the impression that the household chores really are your job and responsibility alone. Or while you might think it's a good thing to offer to help your spouse, that you might actually be sending a mixed message and creating negative feelings.

Challenge #4: "It's never-ending!"

The reality of having demanding jobs and four active kids is that there is never an end to the work that needs to get done around our house. Seriously, Erin and I could work 24/7 and still never finish. But I don't want our home to represent "work." I'm not averse to hard work, but I also need our home to feel like there's room for rest and play. My big fear is that there will never again be downtime in our lives. Not ever.

One of my pet peeves is that we have healthy, able children, but we often fail to get them involved in doing household tasks. I'll come home or be working on something, and Erin will ask me to take care of a simple chore instead of asking one of our kids. This drives me crazy, because it's important for the kids to learn responsibility and contribute to the home we all share.

Above all the grace and the gifts that Christ gives to his beloved is that of overcoming self.
Saint Francis of Assisi

Erin says that this happens because it's easier to ask me to handle the chore than it is to ask our kids. She expects she'll be in for an argument or have to take more time to explain the process than to take care of it on her own. But she's busy, so she opts for me!

When this happens in families with kids, it can build resentment that the kids don't help out. And it gives the kids with an unrealistic picture of shared life. How much easier it would be to handle the workload if everybody pitched in, right? I recently read that roly polys live in families, and the baby bugs actually work together to clean up their habitat.[9] It irks me that bugs have more control than I do!

Another outcome from a seemingly infinite job list is the possibility of broken promises or unfinished chores.

This creates a larger problem of general mistrust. When

your word isn't good, when you fail to do what you promised to do, you lose credibility with your spouse. This leads to much bigger issues than an overgrown lawn or a sink full of dishes.

Building trust in a marriage is both foundational and biblical. Being unified as a Christian couple isn't just a nice thing to be. It's not about defining your roles and then never having to work through basic household issues again. It is actually a spiritual matter. Avoiding petty arguments and passive-aggressive standoffs is vital to living out the biblical model of a loving marriage.

> *Winning is losing when a couple is unable to submit to each other in love.*

Winning is losing when a couple is unable to submit to each other in love and unity.

Author and leader Francis Chan wrote it's a matter of following Christ, summing up the dilemma:

> Arguments escalate when we want to be right more than we want to be Christ. It is easy to get blinded in the heat of disagreements. Soon, all we want is to win, even if victory requires sin. The one who wins the argument is usually the one who acts less like Christ.[10]

MOVING TOWARD SERVICE IN YOUR MARRIAGE

In the end, "how" you divide the household responsibilities (the process) is more important than the ultimate solutions you come up with. The following guidelines will help you hold together as a couple when dividing the chores tries to tear you apart.

1. Be equally responsible for managing your life together. Dividing up household responsibilities begins with a clear mindset: We are *both* equally responsible for our home—inside and outside. We're a team and we need to function like one.

2. Don't just wait for an opening then offer to help. Instead of asking how you can help, take initiative. Don't wait for your spouse to tell you what needs to be done around the house. It's as simple as noticing the dishes are done and need to be unloaded from the dishwasher. Nobody should have to teach a grownup to put dishes away or remind him or her each day that it's important.

> *Marriage becomes a series of surprises for most of us, and one of them is how frequently we need to forgive and be forgiven.*
> Dr. Ed Wheat, *The First Years of Forever*

As Erin and I talked about our own problems in this area, her biggest desire was for me to take initiative—not to wait on her to tell me what needs to be done around the house. Reaching that understanding was a "win" for her.

For me, my "win" is having some down time as a family each night. It's important we have margins in our lives to relax, hang out, and pursue those things that help us rest and relax. So down time is a priority for me.

One way that we've incorporated both of our "wins" into a solution is that I take the initiative to load the dishes into the dishwasher at the end of the night and then I unload them right before I take the kids to school in the morning. I love this system, because I don't feel like we're doing dishes all day long. And it's one less thing that Erin has to worry about.

3. Try to out-serve your spouse. Built upon the foundation of equal ownership, our job is to out-serve our spouse every day. "For even the Son of Man did not come to be served, but to serve" (Mark 10:45).

Take your service to the deepest level and give of your time and energy sacrificially. This means that when I come home after a busy day at work, I jump in and do whatever needs to be done right away. It's not only my responsibility, but it's an opportunity to serve my wife and go the extra mile.

> Take your service to the deepest level and give of your time and energy sacrificially.

Author George Eliot said it well: "What do we live for, if it is not to make life less difficult for each other?"[11]

4. Express gratitude stemming from empathy. Make it a habit to thank your spouse for the work he or she regularly does. Be specific, and if you have children, make sure they hear you praising your spouse and being grateful. It's a good example to set for them, and it reminds them that things around the house don't just get done by magical elves who labor while you're sleeping.

5. Talk about your expectations and preferences. Be willing (like the song says) to "let it go" if it's causing division. Strike a balance between a clean, neat home and a "sanitized for your protection" home.

Remember that some spouses do more housework because they prefer cleaner homes or want something cleaned a certain way. This is where good communication comes in. Be aware of your personal cleanliness preferences (think of all the different ways there are to change sheets, wash the floors, or clean/disinfect a counter). Negotiate these tasks based on realistic expectations.

You may need to release your spouse to then do the chore his or her way. If this balance is acceptable to your spouse, then call it even and move forward.

6. Divide up responsibilities fairly. How you specifically divide up your particular household chores requires you to have a conversation about expectations as "teammates." Remind your spouse that you are on the same team. Therefore, the only possible solution to the chore wars is one that you both feel great about. Live out Philippians 2:4, "Each of you should look not only to your own interests, but also to the interests of others." In other words, divide up the chores in a way that feels equitable or fair to both people. Discover a win-win.

Take into consideration the timing of each other's body clocks. Some spouses are ticking in the morning, and some don't wind up until the evening. Pressuring a spouse to do a task on your schedule instead of his or hers is a great way to begin an argument.

> *Sharing deadlines will synchronize expectations even if it won't synchronize your body clocks.*

Sharing deadlines will synchronize expectations even if it won't synchronize your body clocks. Keep administration communication flowing so each of you can anticipate which tasks need to be tackled by what time. Tip each other off to important meetings, doctor appointments, workout schedules, and the like. Put it on the calendar and let it go.

7. Don't complain, nitpick, or nag. Write a chore contract, list, or calendar, or find some written way to administrate the chores and errands. Post it in a common area. This is essential for couples in the beginning phases of a chore-war truce.

Hold your tongue if a spouse does a chore differently than you would. But if having the laundry separated and washed in a certain system is a live-or-die proposition, then do the laundry yourself.

Be willing to lay aside traditional gender roles. The division of labor in the household often still falls within traditional spheres of "masculine" and "feminine" chores. Erin does a fair share of lawn care, and as I already mentioned, I've taken on dishwasher duty.

A PLANK IN GREG'S EYE APPOINTMENT

One time Greg and I got in a heated argument because he assumed I'd be available to take him to and pick him up from an out-patient eye surgery appointment. He also expected that I'd have time to pick him up from a men's Bible study across town and had a meeting at work. He didn't take into consideration that I was already having to cart around several kids to multiple schools that morning. His communication was poor, and as a result, he had to scramble and ask a friend to take him and pick him up. This was frustrating! I value his Bible studies. I wanted to be with him before and after his surgery, but I just couldn't do it all, especially last minute.

After calmly talking it through, we were able to find a win-win solution. A friend dropped off the kids for me, so I was available to take Greg to the appointment. Communication was key.

This is the final takeaway: you can only change yourself; you can't change your spouse. *Realistic* is your goal, not *perfectionistic*. If you can't gain perspective, consider hiring someone to do those tasks that aren't getting done. Or—gasp!—let your standards slide or give up a task altogether. But do make sure the roof won't fall in—I'm not talking being slothful. Cleaning the bathroom only once a week instead of daily might just be the best way to serve your spouse. Or showing fifteen seconds of respect by rinsing your dishes might win your spouse's heart.

When you both are *100 percent responsible* for the household, when you divide up the regular chores with a teammate mentality, and when your goal is to out-serve the other, you can put an end to the chore wars.

And next time you bring a huge suitcase full of stinky clothes home from vacation, maybe you'll fight each other for the honor of dragging it upstairs.

ROMANCE SECRET #10

TRUE LOVE ENDURES

I have told you all this so that you may have peace in me.
Here on earth you will have many trials and sorrows.
But take heart, because I have overcome the world.
John 16:33, NLT

Set in the upstate New York wilderness during the French and Indian war, the 1992 movie *The Last of the Mohicans* shows us one tough couple: Hawkeye, a raised-by-Indians* long-rifle sniper hero, and Cora, the beautiful, brave, and previously pampered daughter of Colonel Edmund Monroe. In the course of a few days, the war brings the couple many challenges.

In the big-picture view, their fate is intertwined with four opposing forces: the British army, the French army, the Indians, and the pioneer settlers. But primarily their lives are entangled by the evil revenge plans of Magua, a bad-tempered Huron

---

* I apologize for using this term instead of Native American, but it's the language used in the 1820s when the book by the same title was written.

who is obsessed with Cora. He would just as soon burn her at the stake as marry her. Either way, he is determined to make her suffer.

Throughout most of the movie Cora and Hawkeye agree on one thing: they desire a life together, preferably a long one. To make that happen, they have to somehow endure a series of crises: Indians on the warpath, random sniper fire, onslaught by French soldiers, kidnappings, firing squads, taking an arrow through the heart, being burned at the stake, and falling off high cliffs.

What can't be cured must be endured.

John Adams in a letter to his wife, Abigail

At a pivotal moment of the movie, Hawkeye realizes he must leave Cora, who will then most certainly fall into the hands of Magua. Just before they have their fateful night parting, the couple stand in a cave as a waterfall cascades behind them. The rugged frontiersman shouts to his British beauty above the noise of the rushing water: "You be strong, you survive . . . You stay alive, no matter what occurs! I will find you. No matter how long it takes, no matter how far, I will find you."[1]

Like John and Stasi Eldredge, I believe that every couple lives "in a great love story, set in the midst of war."[2]

Let me explain what I mean by "midst of war." It means a crisis or a foreign force acting on your marriage—it's not fighting between spouses. In "Romance Secret #4: True Love Fights for Peace," I used the term *conflict* to describe internal strife, or spouse-versus-spouse issues. The term *crisis* refers to an "external" issue. Marriage crises come in many forms: cancer, disability, in-laws, job loss, financial failures, infidelity, the loss of a child, and so on. It is the couple versus everything or anyone else. In the case of Hawkeye and Cora, it was basically the entire New World universe coming against them.

When a crisis hits your home, what do you do to protect your marriage? What do you expect as the outcome?

When Erin and I are confronted with a crisis, we pull together—and we expect to grow from the experience, no matter how arduous. *Whoa, Greg,* you might be thinking, *I expect to take tranquilizers or a vacation after a crisis, but what do you mean "grow from the experience"?*

I already showed you how an argument can be broken down into these crazy, counterintuitive formulas:

RELATIONSHIP FRICTION + INSIGHT =
INTIMACY INFORMATION

INTIMACY INFORMATION + HEALTHY COMMUNICATION =
HAPPY MARRIAGE

Conflict management can actually help you build intimacy once you learn how to resolve issues.

In the same way, surviving a marriage crisis is not only possible, but those difficult times can also be redeemed by God and transformed into experiences that will strengthen your marriage. Although painful, working through a crisis can force you to grow as an individual. Then you will have the maturity to confront

and fix other problems in your relationship, perhaps issues you
have been "stuck" on for years. The process looks like this:

CRISIS + INSIGHT = PERSONAL GROWTH

PERSONAL GROWTH + CONFLICT RESOLUTION
= STRONGER MARRIAGE

Here's a list of situations that can create a crisis in marriage.
Check the ones that you and your spouse have already faced
over the course of your marriage.

- ❑ death of a loved one
- ❑ child with a disability
- ❑ caring for an elderly parent
- ❑ miscarriage
- ❑ natural disaster
- ❑ job stress
- ❑ infidelity
- ❑ infertility
- ❑ retirement
- ❑ a move
- ❑ sexual difficulties
- ❑ trouble with in-laws
- ❑ loss of a job and/or financial setback
- ❑ physical or mental illnesses
- ❑ spiritual attack
- ❑ war
- ❑ beginning college or a graduate program
- ❑ career setback
- ❑ new life phase[3]

If you've ever faced one of these crises, then you and your spouse are veterans and have already developed some strength and wisdom from experience. In the sections that follow, I'm going to present what I believe are the hallmarks of couples who know how to endure, to agree on a vision, to pull together to meet crises successfully, and to come out stronger.

STRONG COUPLES KNOW CRISIS IS THE NORM

Strong couples don't consider it strange when trials beset them. They know that life contains many places akin to the psalmist's "valley of the shadow of death." But they know these dangerous places come between every peak in life. The couple may have strong emotional reactions when the crisis hits, and they may even be caught off guard, but they are not surprised. Even as a single man, the apostle Paul knew this truth. He wrote, "Those who marry will face many troubles in this life" (1 Corinthians 7:28).

At the beginning of *The Last of the Mohicans*, Cora is a newcomer to the wilderness. She is shocked to find a pioneer settlers' homestead burned to the ground, the bodies of women and children left in the open meadow. By the final scene, she has experienced just about every problem 1757 has to offer except smallpox, but if that, too, hit the feisty heroine, you get the feeling she'd be ready.

Strong Couples Stick It Out
The colonial times Adamses (Abigail and John, not Morticia and Gomez) endured fifty-four years of "for better or for worse" and

had more "worse" than many couples will in this century. They knew the kind of strength God promises in Romans 5:3-5 that

> We also rejoice in our sufferings, because we know that suffering produces perseverance; perseverance, character; and character, hope. And hope does not disappoint us,

---

PROFILES IN MARRIAGE COURAGE

I've been intrigued by a book our daughter Murphy read in high school: *Profiles in Courage,* the 1957 Pulitzer-prize winning book written by John F. Kennedy. The book chronicles the careers of eight American senators who acted courageously and with integrity under tough opposition. These men made choices that they felt were best at the cost of their reputation and favor inside their political party.

The book is written in the spirit of the Hebrews Hall of Fame, the list of great men and women of faith (Hebrews 11). I appreciate stories of heroes because I need reminders that if others can do it, I can do it too.

In the area of marriage, there's one couple I would add to a book about marriage courage: Abigail and John Adams. They lived through the American Revolution. Trials were their life—death, disease, poverty, separation, and political ostracism followed them throughout their marriage. They knew the verse: "Dear friends, do not be surprised at the painful trial you are suffering, as though something strange were happening to you" (1 Peter 4:12).

Abigail and John lived through one of the most bloody periods of our country's history. They documented their woes in thousands of letters. Here's but one of those letters that Abigail wrote to John on October 1, 1775. (I decided it seemed more authentic to leave it uncorrected.)

---

because God has poured out his love into our hearts by the Holy Spirit, whom he has given us.

How does that kind of character help sustain a marriage? Even if you're unhappy now and thinking of calling it quits, or you feel trapped in a loveless marriage, stick it out. Endurance

---

Weymouth october 1 1775

Have pitty upon me, have pitty upon me o! thou my beloved for the Hand of God presseth me soar.

Yet will I be dumb and silent and not open my mouth becaus thou o Lord hast done it.

How can I tell you (o my bursting Heart) that my Dear Mother has Left me, this day about 5 oclock she left this world for an infinitely better.

After sustaining 16 days severe conflict nature fainted and she fell asleep. Blessed Spirit where art thou? At times I almost am ready to faint under this severe and heavy Stroke, seperated from <u>thee</u> who used to be a comfortar towards me in affliction, but blessed be God, his Ear is not heavy that he cannot hear, but he has bid us call upon him in time of Trouble.

I know you are a sincere and hearty mourner with me and will, pray for me in my affliction. . . .

Tis a dreadful time with this whole province. Sickness and death are in almost every family. I have no more shocking and terible Idea of any Distemper except the Plague than this.

Almighty God restrain the pestilence which walketh in darkness and wasteth at noon day and which has laid in the dust one of the dearest of parents. May the Life of the other be lengthend out to his afflicted children and Your distressd Portia*[4]

---

*Abigail signed her letters with a nickname.

pays off. Here's why: Two-thirds of unhappily married spouses who stayed married reported that their marriages were happy five years later. In addition, the most unhappy marriages reported the most dramatic turnarounds: among those who rated their marriages as very unhappy, almost eight out of ten who avoided divorce were happily married five years later.[5]

Erin has some friends who fit this description, Arianna and J. J. Withers. She met them by chance in the park one summer evening. Erin tells the story . . .

As Arianna and J. J.'s twin sons played with Taylor and Murphy on the slides and swings, I sat at a picnic table with the Withers shelling pistachios. J. J. was particularly depressed, and the couple was thinking about splitting up so that Arianna wouldn't have to deal with his anger. They had gotten off to a poor start in their marriage because Arianna got pregnant their senior year in college, "forcing" them to get married. J. J., especially, felt trapped.

Here it was five years later and neither had a career, and they had all but let go of their dreams. They were paying bills day-by-day, switching jobs every eighteen months, feeling as if they were stuck, and that their youth was being flushed down the toilet. J. J. admitted that recently his temper was getting out of control; he'd put a fist through the drywall in the twins' room after they'd put Play-Doh into the swamp cooler.

I encouraged them to stay the course, that really it would only make things worse if J. J. left. But I also knew they had to deal with J. J.'s anger immediately. I asked him to meet with Greg, and they had breakfast the next Saturday morning. Greg challenged J. J. to pull it together, to stop looking back and to move forward. He told him you can't see where you're going if your eyes are on the rearview mirror. It wasn't the marriage that was trapping him, but his mindset that he had somehow been cheated.

I follow them now on Facebook. J. J. got an MBA, they moved, and he's now making plenty of money working for a soft drink company in Atlanta. Arianna sent me a FB message the other day thanking me for encouraging them to stay together four years before. She loves being a mom (their fourth child is on the way), and J. J. is "back to normal," more like the happy, optimistic man she met in college.

Strong Couples Rebuild Trust After a Breach

Trust isn't something that is final in a marriage; it must be rebuilt every day. "The name of the LORD is a fortified tower; the righteous run to it and are safe" (Proverbs 18:10).

Remember my friend Geoff from "Romance Secret #3"? He reconciled with his wife after his "Bathsheba debacle." The infiltration of the other woman was the crisis. Geoff and his wife searched their hearts to find insight, growth, forgiveness, healing, and then strength. It took awhile for his wife to trust him, but his confession went a long way toward opening the doors. She knew he truly wanted to come clean, and that helped her let go of bitterness.

> *Trust isn't something that is final in a marriage; it must be rebuilt every day.*

STRONG COUPLES RECOGNIZE
THE REAL ENEMY

Just as the Smalleys do—and every other couple for that matter—you will face hardship, you will face suffering, you will face opposition, and you will face a multitude of attacks from our sworn enemy.

John and Stasi Eldredge wrote this about the chief enemy of marriage in their book *Love & War*:

> Marriage is hard. It is hard because it is *opposed*. The devil hates marriage; he hates the beautiful picture of Jesus and his Bride that it represents. He hates love and life and beauty in all its forms. The world hates marriage. It hates unity and faithlessness and monogamy. Our flesh is not our ally here either—it rebels when we put others before ourselves. Our flesh hates dying.[6]

Satan's strategy seems to be to keep us oblivious to the bigger picture that was mentioned at the beginning of the chapter: our marriage is a love story, set in the midst of war. If we don't understand this deep in our hearts, we fall right into Satan's second strategy, which is to get us fighting each other so he can "divide and conquer."

> *We need God and we need each other—desperately.*

Your spouse is not the enemy! Satan is the enemy, "Be self-controlled and alert. Your enemy the devil prowls around like a roaring lion looking for someone to devour. Resist him" (1 Peter 5:8-9). Our marriage has a tirelessly engaged enemy who wants to "kill, steal and destroy" our relationship with God and each other. You must maintain a united front that says, "We're in this together! We need God and we need each other—desperately."

ENDURING COUPLES TRUST GOD

The prophet Malachi tells the Israelites what God says, "I hate divorce" (Malachi 2:16). God cares about marriage. Let me rephrase that thought too: God cares about *your* marriage. If you doubt that, meditate on the following scriptures with your spouse and individually:

- Cast all your anxiety on him because he cares for you. (1 Peter 5:7)
- God is faithful; he will not let you be tempted beyond what you can bear. But when you are tempted, he will also provide a way out so that you can stand up under it. (1 Corinthians 10:13)
- God is our refuge and strength, an ever present help in trouble. (Psalm 46:1)
- And we know that in all things God works for the good of those who love him, who have been called according to his purpose. (Romans 8:28)

Let me remind you of Janine and Bertie Harris's story from "Romance Secret #7." The part I didn't tell you about was how Janine grew strong enough to endure the tough times. Early in her marriage, she attended women's events and Bible studies at church. Janine fell in love with Scripture. She posted index cards decorated with positive Bible verses and taped them up all around the house. She bought pillows, pictures, blankets, stationery, coffee mugs, T-shirts, and jewelry with scriptures on them. Eventually, Bertie began to think differently because everywhere he looked at home, a Bible verse was waiting to be read, waiting to comfort him.

If you need to build your faith as a couple, consider joining a couples' Sunday school class, small group, or do a home Bible study together.

Strong Couples Pray

I believe you should pray individually and with your spouse. Erin and I have worked on this over the years. We touch base in the evenings and pray for our family. We pray together as a family also. When we're at church and are asked to pray, our family members seek one another out to hold hands.

God promises to give you wisdom if you ask for it in faith through prayer. So, what are you waiting for? Here are some verses that may inspire you:

- Commit your works to the LORD and your plans will be established. (Proverbs 16:3, NASB)
- Be anxious for nothing, but in everything by prayer and supplication with thanksgiving let your requests be made known to God. And the peace of God, which surpasses all comprehension, will guard your hearts and your minds in Christ Jesus. Finally, brethren, whatever is true, whatever is honorable, whatever is right, whatever is pure, whatever is lovely, whatever is of good repute, if there is any excellence and if anything worthy of praise, dwell on these things. The things you have learned and received and heard and seen in me, practice these things,

and the God of peace will be with you. (Philippians 4:6-9, NASB)

- But if any of you lacks wisdom, let him ask of God, who gives to all generously and without reproach, and it will be given to him. But he must ask in faith without any doubting. (James 1:5-6, NASB)

Strong Couples Keep Their Hearts Open

There's a myth in our culture that says, "I'm not in love with you anymore so I'm free to leave you." Please hear me when I say that "love" is not the issue—we have access to that in abundance through God. Keeping an open heart to allow God's love to flow through us is the first and foremost job of any spouse. (See the sections Managing Conflict in Healthy Ways and Clamming Up Versus Mortal Combat in "Romance Secret #4.")

> *More marriages might survive if the partners realized that sometimes the better comes after the worse.*
>
> Doug Larson, cartoonist and columnist

The real issue is a closed or hardened heart. Let me put it this way: Jesus did *not* say, "Moses permitted you to divorce your wives because . . . *you're not in love with her . . . or your needs aren't being met . . . or you've found someone new.*" He in fact said this was the reason for divorce: "because your hearts were hard" (Matthew 19:8).

Let me tell you about one person I met at the National

Institute of Marriage. This was back in 1999 when MSN first offered its instant messaging service, and Bradley Peterson didn't know the message history could be automatically saved. He found out the hard way when his wife, Olive, discovered a series of illicit conversations stored on the family computer.

I can tell you this, Olive didn't feel very much "in love" with Bradley, especially because she had proof that he was "in love" with someone else.

After a few sessions of individual counseling, Olive decided not to shut down her heart and close off her husband. Instead, she opened her heart to the idea of forgiveness, giving Bradley a second chance. First, she had to trust him when he said the IMs and phone calls were all he had shared with a woman who lived 1,500 miles away. After that, Olive's trust extended to Bradley every day, because with each new gadget or app introduced to the general market, her husband had a new opportunity to seek out someone else on the sly. She felt that even if she earned a degree in information technology, there would be no way she could police him, because even then he could write a letter with paper and pen and there'd not be a trace of incriminating electronic evidence.

> The real battle is to keep your heart open and guard against apathy and hardness.

But Olive doesn't have to worry anymore about digital or carbon-based infidelity. Because of the healing and opening of communication that took place between her and Bradley, they've been able to reestablish trust.

Olive learned that she couldn't control love, but she *could* control the state of her heart. She trusted God to do the rest.

Strong couples guard their hearts from closing, and that way they keep from falling "into trouble" (Proverbs 28:14). The real battle is to keep your heart open and guard against apathy and hardness. Focusing on your own personal growth as an individual is probably the single most important thing you can do to save or improve your marriage. Erin and I will show you how to do this in the next chapter, "Romance Secret #11: True Love Looks Inward."

Strong Couples Follow a Vision

At the opening of *The Last of the Mohicans*, Cora and Hawkeye might seem like opposites because he was a frontiersman who wore leather stockings and she was from Boston and wore silk ones. Though their outside appearances were different, it only took a few scenes to establish what really connected them besides physical attraction: the call of the American dream, with its freedom, autonomy, and individualism. Upon hearing Hawkeye describe the people who live in the wilderness, she said, "It is more deeply stirring to my blood than any imagining could possibly have been."[7] From that moment on, Hawkeye is captivated through their shared passion for independence.

If your marriage could be stronger, perhaps you need a paradigm shift. Don't try to seal up holes in a rowboat if what you really need is a sailboat. Don't work on the relationship you have; instead, build something new, something that thrills you both. Jesus told the Pharisees to put new wine into new wineskins,[8] not old ones—this is the same idea.

Strong Couples Fight Negative Beliefs

I believe most conflict is due to misunderstanding. Strong couples stop making negative assumptions and replace them with curiosity. Give your spouse the benefit of the doubt. Recognize your mate's value. Ask questions because that will most likely keep you from jumping into judgment mode.

If Erin and I had understood how to do this, we would have never experienced Hurricane O. I should have asked her, "Honey, why don't you want to swim?" instead of assuming *She doesn't want to be with me.* I would have found out that Erin is prone to "catastrophizing," that is turning over the possibilities in her mind that everything could turn into a disaster. I've since learned to be patient when she is presented with a potentially threatening scenario.

Erin says that she's also learned to give me the benefit of the doubt:

> When Greg bought the Ms. Pac-Man machine, for example, I might have assumed he did it because he was out to get me for sometimes caring too much what the house looks like, that he was selfish and insensitive to the core. But when I asked him why he'd bought it, he told me that he thought it would remind me of California. Once I was able to see his heart, I knew that he really had, at some bizarre primordial level, been trying to reconnect with the early days of our relationship. A Red Robin gift card would have sufficed.

Strong Couples Celebrate Differences

Strong couples learn to accept differences as good things. I've come to rely on Erin to help me judge what's best for the kids. Her background as a nurse came in handy this week after

Garrison sprained his ankle. On the other side of the coin, she says that as a family, we have more fun because I'm willing to seek adventure more often than she would. Sure, we've had conflict over that, but overall we are now more centered, appreciating the differences each of us brings to the marriage table.

> *Expect trouble as an inevitable part of life and when it comes ... look it squarely in eye and say, "I will be bigger than you."*
> Ann Landers, advice columnist and author

We've also learned to accept each other's limitations. You must realize that in order to be happy with your spouse, you don't necessarily have to like every single thing about him or her. You have to accept that's just part of marriage. Most couples never resolve most of their key problems. And if they leave the marriage union, they'd most likely find different but equally upsetting and unfixable problems with the next person.

While I appreciate Erin's sense of responsibility, I know sometimes it can't be mitigated, and that is frustrating. Remember the 2014 Ebola scare? Well, they could have put Erin in charge of that

> *Overcoming the differences in your personalities turns you into a team.*

whole operation, and that virus would have been shaking to the core of its lipid membrane. I believe she's capable of outthinking and outplanning just about anyone. At home, it's her first reaction to keep the kids and me from harm. It's my last. She's not going to change, but I don't let it set me off like it used to in the honeymoon phase.

Overcoming the differences in your personalities turns you into a team. So, you either win or lose together. There is no such thing as a win-lose arrangement because you are on the same team, and if your spouse loses, inevitably so do you.

STRONG COUPLES SEEK HELP

Please don't do marriage alone. Seek out other couples who believe in marriage and will support you as you seek to establish a unifying vision. If you're in trouble or merely not thriving as a couple, seek counseling, marriage seminars, books, videos, or other resources. Surround yourselves with supportive people, knowing that, "A friend loves at all times, and a brother is born for a time of adversity" (Proverbs 17:17, NIV, 2011).

Strong couples set aside a time weekly to talk about how things are going in their relationship. (See "Romance Secret #7: True Love Needs Time to Grow.") Talk about any issues that arise or emotions you are feeling. Schedule this time in the office of a counselor if you need help to ensure these discussions are productive and don't escalate into blame games or arguments.

STRONG COUPLES REMINISCE

A friend's father had a stroke last month. She went to stay with her parents to provide moral and practical support. She brought along a tape recorder and taped more than six hours of their marriage memories. Sure they squabbled a bit now and again about a certain detail—"No, it was Aunt Agnes, not Ruth who brought the tomato aspic"—but overall they were giddy talking about their courtship, honeymoon, and times when they lived abroad in Air Force housing.

Charity certainly means one of two things—pardoning unpardonable acts, or loving unlovable people.

G.K. Chesterton, *Orthodoxy*

Focus on the Acts 14:27 moments. This verse says, "[The disciples] gathered [at] the church together and reported all that God had done through them and how he had opened the door of faith to the Gentiles." When you've got a few minutes, rehearse what you will say when you're in your eighties and one of your children asks you what your marriage was like.

STRONG COUPLES CULTIVATE HOPE

Okay, spoiler time. Don't read what's next if you've not seen *The Last of the Mohicans* but are planning to.

In one of the near-final scenes of the movie, all seems lost for Cora and her sister, Alice. They are on a craggy mountain trail, being forced to walk the treacherous trail by Magua and his kin.

Uncas, a young Mohican friend of Hawkeye attacks Magua, seeking to free the women. He fights valiantly, but perishes at the hand of Magua. Alice despairs and stands at the edge of a cliff as if to jump. As Magua tries to coax her back to safety, she defiantly jumps off the ledge—giving up hope.

Cora, who is now near broken, her heart rent from watching

her sister fall, remains with her enemies. And in the next scene Hawkeye defies all odds and frees her with the help of Uncas's father, now the last Mohican.

Couples, take heart. Be strong and courageous when you feel surrounded by the enemy.[9] And you will be surrounded, that's a sure bet. But here's an even greater certainty for you to cling to: "If we died with him, we will also live with him; if we endure, we will also reign with him . . . he will remain faithful" (2 Timothy 2:11-13).

Up next, "Romance Secret #11: True Love Looks Inward," on dealing with your own part of the problem and how God can help you love your spouse in spite of yourself.

For special date night ideas and discussion questions, you can visit *crazylittlethingcalledmarriage.com.*

TRUE LOVE
LOOKS INWARD

I have counsel and sound wisdom;
I have insight; I have strength.
—Proverbs 8:14, ESV

Set during the bleak 1930s, the award-winning film *Seabiscuit* is a true story about a temperamental racehorse and his remarkable ability to win against all odds, inspiring not only the racing world but also a despairing nation under economic siege.

As a foal, Seabiscuit is not an obvious champion; he is undersized and unfocused. None of his trainers can get him to run well; one of them, in exasperation, orders a jockey to whip Seabiscuit into shape. The brutality yields aggression rather than speed. The thoroughbred is now undersized, unfocused, ferociously uncooperative, and for sale.

As new owners Mr. and Mrs. Howard watch Seabiscuit

sprint on a racecourse, they see the athletic three-year-old weave awkwardly around the track, his rider struggling to keep him in line.

Mrs. Howard remarks, "Seems pretty fast."

The horse's trainer, Tom Smith, embarrassed by the animal's poor performance, looks at the ground and mutters, "Yeah, in every direction."[1]

Smith attributes the horse's problems to the abuse he received at former stables: "[Seabiscuit is] so beat up, it's hard to tell what he's like. I just can't help feelin' they got him so screwed up runnin' in a circle, he's forgotten what he was born to do. He just needs to learn how to be a horse again."[2]

The Howards are encouraged when they see Seabiscuit run gracefully and with passion on an open trail in a meadow—doing what he was created to do. With the care and empathy of Smith and the daring and determination of jockey Johnny "Red" Pollard, Seabiscuit gradually overcomes his distrust and learns to compete on the racetrack despite setbacks and fierce competition. It took awhile, but Seabiscuit accepted his birthright and became the champion he was bred to be.[3]

Like Seabiscuit, every person is saddled with unhappy memories and scars from being mistreated. Many have been so beat up and wounded that it's difficult at times to see their true potential. Their God-given gifts have been overlooked, and their honest natures have been twisted out of shape.

Today's culture has many married people so confused they are running in relationship circles. Some have lost sight of what they were born to do—what they were created to do—so they no longer understand their purpose. And without that realization, they can't hope to have the thriving marriages God has planned for them.

Do you remember how your purpose was defined in "This Thing Called Love"? Your marriage destiny is "to love."

> *In marriage do thou be wise: prefer the person before money, virtue before beauty, the mind before the body; then thou hast a wife, a friend, a companion, a second self.*
>
> William Penn, *Some Fruits of Solitude*

Throughout this book I've been encouraging you to do just that. This chapter could easily have been positioned as "Romance Secret #2"—but I've saved it for near the end because I want you to understand the scope and depth of the commitment God is calling you to strive toward.

No spouse, not even the best, can do these things—nourish, cherish, unite, communicate, endure, embrace—in his or her own power. The secret to loving well is first being transformed by God; only then can you truly serve your spouse.

Let's look at the greatest commandments in Jesus' words again: "'Love the Lord your God with all your heart and with all your soul and with all your mind.' This is the first and greatest commandment. And the second is like it: 'Love your neighbor as yourself'" (Matthew 22:37-39).

By putting God first with your entire being, God honors

you by working through you. God wants your hearts abundantly full of His love so you can share His love with others. That's why the apostle Paul wrote to the church at Thessalonica, "May the Lord make your love increase and overflow for each other and for everyone else, just as ours does for you" (1 Thessalonians 3:12).

Love Overflowing

If there's a love shortage, it isn't on God's end. His love is forever available, abounding even. It is higher than the heavens; conquers the grave, keeps us from slipping, and fills the earth—literally.[4]

There's one biblical image in particular I want you to have in your mind when it comes to love. God's love is a fountain of life with living waters flowing from it.[5] Such a fountain is necessary for marital happiness. Take a look at King Solomon's words in Proverbs 5:18: "May your fountain be blessed, and may you rejoice in the wife of your youth." I believe this blessed fountain represents love being poured out in marriage.[6] Just as the body needs water for survival, your relationship needs love in order to thrive.

Problem Children

If your spring of love dries up, then you'll have trouble. This potential problem involves people like you and me, flawed individuals. Each one of us is, at times, God's problem child. Spouses interfere with God's love flowing through them when they shut off the love fountain. This is why King Solomon also wrote, "Above all else, guard your heart, for it is the wellspring of life" (Proverbs 4:23).

In case you didn't notice, this phrase, "above all else," isn't just a transition to make the verse sound official or poetic. It really means first, foremost, number one, and top priority. It is vital to keep your heart flowing God's love to others. Don't ignore this profound yet simple truth.

I know you're asking, *So, Greg, what makes a person's heart dry up? What stops individuals from fulfilling the purposes God has intended for them?*

Some of the potential reasons were presented in "Romance Secrets #4, #6, and #10," and the things that cause conflict and/or attack your marriage can also affect your wellspring of life. If you are fatigued, you can't offer your spouse what you don't have. (Review those three Secrets if you feel you need to.) In this chapter, however, I want to focus on one specific reason your love fountain can dry up: You're trapped in sin, holding onto "stuff" you just can't release.

> If you are fatigued, you can't offer your spouse what you don't have.

WHAT'S YOUR MONKEY TRAP?

A series of fables, dating as far back as Aesop in the sixth century BC, warn about being trapped by an unwillingness to let go. In India, the legend revolves around "the monkey trap," which refers to a hollowed out coconut tethered to the ground or to a tree. The shell has a single opening just large enough to fit a monkey's small, flexible hand.

To load the trap, bait is placed into the coconut—a slice of fruit or some other delicacy to tempt a monkey. A curious and hungry monkey reaches into the tethered coconut and clenches its fist around the bait. But when it tries to pull its hand out, its fist is too big to get through the opening with the bait still clenched in his hand.

So what does the monkey do? Sadly, the monkey refuses to let go of the bait, to his detriment.

Clearly it's not the coconut that traps the monkey. Instead, the true snare is the monkey's unwillingness to let go of the prize.

Many of us suffer a similar plight. So often in life husbands and wives mentally, emotionally, and spiritually hold onto the very things that trap and imprison them. They refuse to let go of their pursuit of money, pornography, overeating, shopping, or workaholism. Or it might be wounds from the past that they can't let go of (abuse, failure, rape, molestation, being bullied, sexual promiscuity, abortion, etc.). And like the monkey, when they refuse to let go, they get stuck.

Greg's Monkey Trap

I recently went through a four-day personal intensive called Impact Training, which is designed to help individuals understand how they can love others unconditionally. The experience helped me recognize the impact I have on others.

At one point in the intensive, the feedback I received made my head spin with confusion. Over and over, people kept using words like *secretive, hiding, guarded*, and *withholding* to describe me. I didn't know I came across that way. I thought I was as open and friendly as a Labrador retriever puppy.

But over the four days, God revealed a destructive pattern I'd had my entire life. I realized that my monkey trap—what I refused to release—was hiding and keeping secrets. From a young age I'd learned to cover up my mistakes. Instead of facing the consequences of my choices, I hid the things that might embarrass me or get me in trouble.

My mind flooded with examples of my secrets. As a young boy, I hid Little Debbie Swiss Rolls and Nutty Bars in my room so my mom wouldn't catch me eating junk food. In grade school, I hid the fact that I had a learning disability because I was so embarrassed about my poor reading. In high school, I hid a dirty magazine in the attic. In college, I hid a very dark secret from my family and close friends that launched me into severe depression for years: my girlfriend had an abortion. Early in my marriage, I hid cash in a tennis ball can so I wouldn't have to battle Erin over spending money. Over and over, I used the same coping mechanism: hiding.

Love me when I least deserve it because
that is when I really need it.
Swedish proverb

For me, this gave the term *harsh reality* a new meaning. I can't tell you how difficult it was to own up to my monkey trap. My conscience was squirming like a worm washed from the dirt by a good rain.

The pattern that traps me has become so ingrained I often don't even see it. For example, just four days after the Impact Training, Erin and I led a marriage seminar in Florida. The church gave us an amazing gift and put us up at a beachfront resort. At some point over the weekend, Erin asked why I seemed so shut down. I actually had no idea, but I could feel it too. I thought maybe I was just fatigued.

But God is committed to helping free me of my monkey trap, and He used Scripture to show me what I was doing.

The morning of our marriage seminar, I was reflecting on some verses that I'd written down about secrets. I hadn't had time to review the verses since the Impact Training. When I read Psalm 51:6, "Surely you desire truth in the inner parts; you teach me wisdom in the inmost place," the truth hit me. I felt shut down because I had been ogling bikini-clad women on the beach, and I was trying to hide this behavior from Erin by wearing dark sunglasses that shadowed my furtive glances.

Then I read a verse from Job 24 and—there's no other way to say it—*it freaked me out*:

> There are those who rebel against the light, who do not
> know its ways or stay in its paths. . . . The eye of the adul-
> terer watches for dusk; he thinks, "No eye will see me,"
> and he keeps his face concealed. . . . For all of them, deep
> darkness is their morning; they make friends with the ter-
> rors of darkness. (13,15, and 17)

The Holy Spirit and God's Word conspired to stalk my con-science, and I'm thankful for it. My lustful behavior had caused me to shut down—to hide!

Only now am I beginning to fully understand the price I've paid over the years for my secrets. It has cost me my integrity at times—like when I hid money from Erin in a tennis ball can or when I didn't tell her about buying something simple as a DVD or as big as a $3,000 antique—and it has cost me authentic intimacy and deep connection to Erin. She has also had to suffer because I chose to hide.

> *The great news is that God wants to help you let go of whatever you're holding inside your monkey trap.*

The great news is that God wants to help you let go of whatever you're holding inside your monkey trap and then use you to do great things. Second Timothy 2:21 offers this promise: "Therefore, if anyone cleanses himself from what is dishonorable, he will be a vessel for honorable use, set apart as holy, useful to the master of the house, ready for every good work" (ESV).

Letting Go of Your Monkey Trap

But to receive that promise, you have to be willing to change, to cleanse your soul and conscience. To find out if you have a monkey trap, ask yourself these questions:

- What is one thing that is keeping you stuck? What do you need to let go of to experience freedom?
- What is keeping you from being healthier and more joyful? A negative attitude or faulty belief? A lie that Satan has been telling you?
- Are you holding on to bitterness or resentment?
- Is a wound from the past encaging you?
- Is regret of a past mistake keeping you captive?
- Do you hold on to an unhealthy habit? An unhealthy relationship or fantasy life?

A successful marriage requires maturity—that means being able to let go of your monkey traps. Both spouses must be committed to personal growth and development. You don't get to criticize your spouse's behavior or point out what he or she is mistakenly grasping without first looking inward and identifying your own monkey traps. You have to let go first.

> *You can sacrifice and not love. But*
> *you cannot love and not sacrifice.*
>
> Kris Vallotton, author and pastor

Jesus used a different word picture. He summed up that principle using the metaphor of specks and planks: "How can you say to your brother, 'Let me take the speck out of your eye,' when all the time there is a plank in your own eye? You hypocrite, first take the plank out of your own eye, then you will see clearly to remove the speck from your brother's eye" (Matthew 7:4-5).

To be mature means we are *teachable*, able to remove planks. This quality must be intentionally developed. Author and friend Gary Chapman notes that in his counseling sessions he gives the couple paper and pens. He then asks them to list their own faults. Each spouse can usually list only a few things wrong with him- or herself. But when asked to list the faults of their marriage partner, the writers often ask for more paper.[7]

> To be mature means we are teachable, *able to remove planks.*

A mature person is capable of being instructed, trained, and coached by God, a mentor, and his or her spouse. This person can accurately and somewhat objectively see his or her faults for what they are—areas in life that need attention. God calls this process of personal refinement *sanctification*, or becoming Christlike. Second Corinthians 3:18 describes that process like this: "We . . . are being transformed into [Christ's] likeness with ever-increasing glory, which comes from the Lord."

Five Steps to Freedom

How do we journey toward this promised transformation? I've outlined five steps that will help you let go of your monkey trap. Think of each step as a finger you're unclenching to free yourself from the trap.

Step #1: Become aware. Try to understand your "stuff." Don't accept your behavior at face value, but be curious about what causes you to act as you do. This is what Impact Training did for me—it helped reveal my lifelong pattern of hiding.

Step #2: Encounter God's truth. During the training, God's truth was able to sink in. I realized that I didn't want to be hiding anymore because I was not living as the person He created me to be. When you align your life to match biblical teaching, when you strive toward obedience, then your monkey traps no longer have a hold of you. Jesus explained this principle in John 8:31-32: "If you hold to my teaching, you are really my disciples. Then you will know the truth, and the truth will set you free."

This is a twofold step. First you must make sure your heart is open to learning and changing. Second, you must read the Bible. You can't build your faith without exposing your life to God's character-building truth. "All Scripture is breathed out by God and profitable for teaching, for reproof, for correction, and for training in righteousness, that the man of God may be competent, equipped for every good work" (2 Timothy 3:16-17, ESV). "Your word is a lamp to my feet and a light to my path" (Psalm 119:105, ESV). Bottom line? Read your Bible or listen to an audio version if you want a message from God.

Step #3: Practice confessing your sins out loud. First John 1:9 states, "If we confess our sins, he is faithful and just and will forgive us our sins and purify us from all unrighteousness." The Greek word for *confess* is *homologeo*, which was typically used for a public confession; it means "to profess; to declare openly, speak out freely."[8] When you speak a difficult-to-admit truth out loud to God or others, that action creates humility and causes you to accept responsibility or to "own" that truth.

First just admit the wrongdoing aloud in a prayer. Tell your spouse. Tell a trusted mentor (James 5:16). Bring this sin into the light as Ephesians 5:11-14 instructs us: "Take no part in the unfruitful works of darkness, but instead expose them. . . . But when anything is exposed by the light, it becomes visible, for anything that becomes visible is light" (ESV). The experience will help clarify what's right and what's wrong, worthy and unworthy, preparing you for your good works. (See 2 Timothy 2:21 again.)

Step #4: Experience forgiveness. This step follows closely after confession. The normal order of the forgiveness experience is asking God to forgive you. The realization that you've wronged someone or made a general slipup against the Creator usually comes from read-ing the Bible or personal reflection

> *When anything is exposed by the light, it becomes visible.*

after you've encountered friction in a relationship. That's why Jesus included asking for forgiveness in the prayer He taught the disciples to pray.[9] Talking to God about your shortcomings, particularly in regard to your spouse, should be a top priority. But sometimes His grace is difficult to accept; guilt gathers like dust bunnies even after you think you've swept them away. If guilt plagues you, keep 1 John 1:9 somewhere you will see it every day to remind yourself that God does forgive: "If we confess our sins, he is faithful and just and will forgive us our sins and purify us from all unrighteousness."

> *Being loved is life's second greatest*
> *blessing; loving is the greatest.*
> Dr. Jack Hyles, *Blue Denim and Lace*

Next, you may need someone to forgive you. Again, this person is often your spouse because you have so much intimate interaction with your mate. I recently had to apologize to Erin for a joke gone wrong. I didn't mean to burden her—really, no malice aforethought. In fact, I put no "aforethought" at all into my action, and Erin paid the embarrassing price of appearing rude in front of Annie's speech therapist.

The final stage to step #4 is forgiving others. Someone could have wronged you, and you need to forgive him, her, or the organizational entity. This can be a blatant wrongdoing or a subtle slight to your pride. Again, self-reflection (being aware) will bring this to light. The anger part eventually surfaces. The need to share grace, however, is not so easy to detect.

The story that follows is one of Erin's experiences in deep forgiveness.

ERIN'S FORAY INTO FORGIVENESS

Before Greg had his secret life exposed at the Impact Training seminar, I had taken part in one. I went to the event intrigued by what my friends had told me about the experience. I was looking for respite and a glowing sort of self-enlightenment, the adult version of Christian summer camp. I wanted to be wowed. But after the first night, I wanted to come home.

That evening, one of the trainers, who hadn't had any contact with me, told me that I looked exhausted, angry, and bitter. His words came out of the blue, and he left abruptly so I couldn't ask what his comments were all about.

His behavior shot me through the roof. I hadn't thought I was angry, but I fulfilled his expectations—I became infuriated.

I called Greg later that night, and told him, "I'm coming home tomorrow. I'm not staying here."

All night I mulled over the trainer's statement and why I was so miffed about his random assessment. The man reminded me of my father. Both were curt and insensitive. Once memories of my dad came through, I couldn't push the thoughts out of my head. As a child, I'd been the victim of my dad's anger, and here I was, fuming just like he did all the time. I didn't like what I saw in my character. I did not want to pass this anger legacy on to my kids.

After sleeping fitfully, I woke up next morning realizing I had more dad stuff to deal with even though a few months earlier he had offered a heartfelt apology for his rough parenting style. I decided two things: (1) I'd stay at the seminar, and (2) I would ask my dad for forgiveness because I had been carrying pride, thinking I was a better parent than he was and looking down on him.

I wanted a completely healed relationship on my part, and so I called him. It would have been easy to bypass this conversation, but I've learned the value of confessing my "stuff" and the joy of restored relationship.

Step #5: Treasure hunt your pain. Remember the clamshells we talked about in "Romance Secret #4?" Did you know that a clam makes its shell from the same material it makes a pearl? Pain can either cause you to form a shell around your heart, closing it off, or you can make something beautiful from it—dare I say it?—a pearl of wisdom! When hard times come to you, consider diving into the treasure-hunt business. These gems come through the Holy Spirit: love, joy, peace, patience, kindness, goodness, gentleness, faithfulness, self-control,[10] steadfastness, endurance, and hopefulness.

I think James understood this concept well. That's how he was able to write—in all seriousness and without flinching—that trials should be considered *joyful* events. (Wouldn't you be happy if you opened a clamshell and found a pearl?) It took me years to understand this profound passage, but now I've come to understand that God's best gifts are often given in pain-wrapped packages:

> Count it all joy, my brothers, when you meet trials of
> various kinds, for you know that the testing of your faith
> produces steadfastness. And let steadfastness have its full
> effect, that you may be perfect and complete, lacking in
> nothing. (James 1:2-4, ESV)

Here's another verse that refers to joy-infused suffering:

> We rejoice in our sufferings, knowing that suffering produces
> endurance, and endurance produces character, and character
> produces hope, and hope does not put us to shame, because
> God's love has been poured into our hearts through the Holy
> Spirit who has been given to us. (Romans 5:3-5, ESV)

Erin and I compiled a short list of some Smalley treasures that started out as painful:

- Annie's abandonment meant we could adopt her.
- My confession to "hiding" led to a deeper and more authentic intimacy in our marriage.
- Our difficulty managing conflict early in our marriage led us to learn how to work through conflict—so we're pretty good at it now.
- My girlfriend's abortion in college helped me learn to have grace toward others when they make mistakes.
- Erin's mother's death gave her a deeper appreciation for family and friends.
- I didn't get into law school, which allowed me to become a marriage therapist and help marriages.
- Erin and I left Branson, Missouri, and a very difficult family business, which freed us up to move to the Center for Healthy Relationships, and then from there to come to Focus on the Family to lead its marriage department.

Feeling Safe Together

Inward healing draws you closer as a couple because you feel safer—you aren't a threat. When someone has personal issues that aren't being dealt with, it makes them feel unsafe. They may hurt you (anger, rage, passive-aggressiveness), they may not be able to connect with you (depression or anxiety), or they may be needy and demanding that you love them (they feel like a vacuum sucking every time to try to relate or connect). Dealing with your junk makes your spouse feel as if you are safer and less threatening. "It's much easier to connect with you because you seem safe."

The record books show that in 1938 and 1939 Seabiscuit won seventeen of twenty-six races, and either placed or showed in all

---

TIMING IS EVERYTHING

Shortly after our friend Rae got married, she found a hand was caught in a monkey trap. Rae had to let go of feelings that her marriage to Sam wasn't right for her.

After a couple of casual dates with Sam, Rae moved out of state to take a new job in the events industry. She thought the relationship was over. Despite Rae's warnings that she wasn't really ready to get married, and that she wasn't as enthused about him as he was about her, Sam knew he wanted to marry her. He got a job and moved to be near her.

Rae felt that God was calling her to marry Sam. Ignoring some twinges about the timing, when Sam proposed, she said yes. Feelings of doubt about the marriage soon crept in, however. She still had dreams to pursue. Her job took her away for long periods of time and their relationship status was shaky and frustrating. Rae's feelings of being tied down too soon kept her from investing in the marriage.

Sam allowed Rae her freedom, and he was patient. But there came a day when Rae realized they were going to drift so far apart that she might want to leave. Additionally, the lifestyle of the events industry began to wear on her—the atmosphere wasn't exactly wholesome and the travel interrupted daily life with Sam. She wrestled with God and realized she would need to put Sam first, letting go of her job in order to give the marriage the commitment it needed to thrive.

but one of the remaining nine.[11] The highlight of Seabiscuit's career was when he raced War Admiral, a Triple Crown champion, head to head. On November 1, 1938, Franklin D. Roosevelt and forty million other Americans listened to the race on radio. Seabiscuit gave a country hope that the "little guy" could triumph.[12]

The movie *Seabiscuit* clearly shows how this special horse is a treasure to the nation in general and to three damaged individuals in particular. Owner Charles Howard is willing to risk again after the death of his son. Trainer Tom Smith regains his self-respect after losing a career as a cowboy. Jockey Johnny "Red" Pollard finds a home and finally feels valued after being abandoned by his family and being treated poorly by the racing community. In the last line of the movie, he says, "You know, everybody thinks we found this broken-down horse and fixed him, but we didn't. He fixed us. Every one of us. And I guess in a way we kinda fixed each other too."[13]

Having a supportive community is one way we can all get "fixed." The next chapter, "Romance Secret #12: True Love Seeks Fellowship," will help you identify ways to be part of a community that supports marriage.

TRUE LOVE SEEKS FELLOWSHIP

Though one may be overpowered, two can defend
themselves. A cord of three strands is not quickly broken.
Ecclesiastes 4:12

Warning: *This section contains material from The Lord of the Rings. If you've been oversaturated by the six epic movies, and can't stand another mention of the Shire or see another orc slaughtered, stay with me anyway . . . there's a takeaway as illuminating as Galadriel's phial.*

I for one, remain a J. R. R. Tolkien fan because I love a grand adventure and because the themes of self-sacrifice and destiny speak to my soul. (Every Christmas break Garrison and I have a LOTR and Hobbit movies marathon.)

Even though the release of *The Return of the King* movie was more than a decade ago, several spiritual truths I learned from the trilogy still resonate with me. The struggles of Tolkien's characters to defeat the evil Lord Sauron and the evil within themselves have given me inspiration. I see the themes of the legends paralleling marriage and wedding ceremonies.

You see, in both LOTR lore and at weddings, it's all about the Ring. (Didn't see that one coming, did you?)

One of my favorite scenes in the first movie is during the Council of Elrond. It's a beautiful stone patio setting with mature

---

A MARRIAGE COMMITMENT
FROM THE CONGREGATION

My good friend, pastor Ted Cunningham, takes congregational commitment to marriage to a higher level. Here's what he does during the weddings that he officiates at Woodland Hills church in Branson, Missouri.

> We have a greeting card that we've designed, called More Than Wine. On the front, it has the Song of Solomon 1:4, "We rejoice and delight in you, we will praise your love more than wine."
>
> And on in the inside it says, "I desire to bless your marriage by speaking words of high value over both of you. Your marriage is important to me" and "I rejoice, I delight, I praise." So now, when you come to a wedding at Woodland Hills, or a wedding that I do or any of our pastors does, everyone who comes to the wedding gets this card in an envelope.
>
> At the "Welcome," I move the bride and groom to the side and let them just take in the day and the moment while I talk to family and friends and I ask them throughout the day to fill out this card and rejoice in the light and praise and the love of this couple.

trees and an elegant, ancient castle as a picturesque backdrop.
Fall leaves flutter gently from the trees. The Elf-ruler, Elrond,
officiates the council with wise dignity. After some heated discussion, Frodo the humble Hobbit inevitably accepts the call to
serve as the Ring-bearer. The task is going to be a long, arduous
journey; it will most likely end in death. So when a wizard, a
king, an elf, a dwarf, and a seasoned warrior volunteer to accompany Frodo on his journey, my heart stirs. And when his

And I say, "There are three ways to use this card.
Many of you will fill this out today and put it into the 'More
Than Wine' box in the Reception Hall. And during the first
year, the couple's going to reach into the box and pull out
cards all during the year and be encouraged. The second
group of you I want you to 'Hold It' until their first anniversary, and then give it to them." (And then, this is the one
that I love.)

The third group is the parents, the grandparents, the
bridesmaids, the groomsmen, and maybe fifty to sixty
more of you. We want you to hold this card until you hear
that this couple is going through a difficult time, separat-
ing, or divorcing. And then I look over at the couple and
ask them, "Do we have your permission to send you a
hundred of these cards when we hear there's trouble?"
And I make them give me an audible answer. (Similar to
when you're on the exit aisle of an airplane, they make
you give them an audible reply, not just a "nod."). So we
have all of that on tape.

People are getting into these cards. And what I'm
doing now is handing twelve of these cards that have all
the different messaging on them to Mom and Dad and
asking them to send one card each month during the first
year of their child's new marriage.

three best friends finagle their way onto the traveling team—or fellowship as it's called in the lore—the scene is complete.[1]

Now pause and imagine an outdoor wedding ceremony on a similar patio. Recast Elrond in your mind's eye as a wise and dignified reverend wearing a robe (and without the silver headband thing). The bride and groom wait patiently for the service to begin. The dozen or so guests sit in elegant, plush chairs, which are arranged in a semicircle.

> *The man who sanctifies his wife*
> *understands that this is his divinely*
> *ordained responsibility... Is my wife more*
> *like Christ because she is married to me?*
>
> R. Kent Hughes, *Disciplines of a Godly Man*

The Reverend Elrond addresses them somberly and says, "Should anyone here present know of any reason that this couple should not be joined in holy matrimony, speak now or forever hold your peace."

Suddenly, several people in the audience speak out. The bride's former high school guidance counselor says, "I say they shouldn't get married at all! Don't you know 40 percent of all first marriages end in divorce?" The mother of the bride says, "I don't think the groom makes enough money. They'll probably wind up living in my basement. Call it off." The groom's college roommate says, "He looks at porn. She should run before it's too late."

On and on the objections roll in. They're not old enough.

They're not ready for kids. She's a control freak. He's a slob. They don't know what they're getting into.

Even though Reverend Elrond quiets the guests, some are still obviously upset. He turns to the couple. "This is a serious commitment you're making. Do you understand the perils of this marriage adventure—and that it will end only in death?"

The bride and groom nod their heads. They exchange the vows and the rings.

Then Reverend Elrond again turns to the onlookers. He says, "Who will accompany this couple on their life journey and offer aid to their success?"

At first there's silence. Then the best man kneels beside the groom and says, "If by my life or by my death I can protect you, you have my sword!"

Some things sound better in Middle-earth than they do in middle-class America. But the word *fellowship* belongs in every healthy community. In the Bible, *fellowship* connotes a shared vision. It means "community," "intimacy," and "joint participation."[2] The God of this universe created us to be in relationship—with Him and with others. We were never meant to tackle the challenges of life and marriage alone. Couples need a strong community surrounding them at all times—a "fellowship of the wedding rings" so to speak.

> *Couples need a strong community surrounding them at all times.*

That's why I love it when family members and close friends make a vow at the wedding to support the couple. When I'm officiating, I ask the wedding guests, "As a part of the community that surrounds this couple, do you pledge your love and support in keeping this marriage forever strong?"

Asking for this commitment isn't just sentimental jargon. It's my way of alerting the couple's loved ones that the couple needs support, that the community needs to play an active role in their lives.

Why? Because marriage is difficult. Satanic forces greater than any fantasy-book enemy will try to break the couple's commitment. And each person's innate self-centeredness is bound to create problems in a marriage. Even the healthiest relationships go through conflict, disappointment, and temptation. So family and friends have a continuing role in the couple's grand adventure. This is the moment that our loved ones, who vowed to support and fight for our marriage, can make the difference between relationship life and death. Their shared participation shouldn't end after they drop off the gift and a card at the reception.

THREE TYPES OF FELLOWSHIP CIRCLES

Erin and I desperately needed Christian friends to boost us when we were struggling. When we first got married, we were euphoric, bubbling over with an it's-just-you-and-me-against-the-world! attitude. And when that became it's-you-and-me-against-each-other! attitude, we didn't know how to ask for help.

We noted in "Romance Secret #9: True Love Serves" that unity is essential for a strong marriage. But a couple also needs Christian community or fellowship with like-minded friends. This is a two-way street: the couple needs the church and the church needs them. To be strong, a couple needs to give and to take. God's Word directs all of us to "consider how we may spur one another on toward love and good deeds. Let us not give up meeting together, as some are in the habit of doing, but let us encourage one another" (Hebrews 10:24-25). Married couples are an integral part of the church community.

> *Picture marriage as a vehicle for mission, an opportunity for Christians to carry out our mission to make disciples of all the nations.*
>
> Francis Chan, *You and Me Forever*

A relational God created us for fellowship, for joining in beneficial relationships, the iron-sharpening-iron process described in Proverbs 27:17. Spouses who share a healthy, vibrant relationship rely on their support system, but they also recognize that they have a responsibility to help other couples thrive. Community is a part of our DNA. We were designed to know and be known by our spouse and to a more limited extent by the community. A spouse alone is not enough to fulfill our deep desire for fellowship. By experiencing married life in healthy community, a couple realizes multiple benefits—benefits documented in a variety of research studies.[3]

> *A spouse alone is not enough to fulfill our deep desire for fellowship.*

How should you build and maintain a strong support system? How can you contribute to the health of other couples' marriages? Erin and I recommend finding friends in three categories.

1. Mentor Couples

Gary and Carrie Oliver were the first mentors Erin and I had. Unfortunately we didn't meet with them until we'd been arguing for a while. And we didn't ask for their help—we were so dysfunctional the Olivers had to step into our lives. It all began because we needed groceries.

We were living in Englewood, Colorado, and I was, ironically, a graduate student in counseling at Denver Seminary. Talk about the blind leading the blind!

One afternoon Erin left our apartment to shop, and Carrie just happened to call. I picked up the phone and said hello.

"Hi, Greg," Carrie said. "Is Erin there?"

I was depressed, distracted, and distant because I'd been working and she'd interrupted me. I managed to say, "Uh, she's gone."

There was a long silence. Then Carrie said, "Greg, I am so sorry. We've been so worried about you two. Are you going to be okay?"

Her question confused me. "What are you talking about?" I asked. "Erin is at King Soopers market."

There was a long pause, long enough for even an ox like me to figure out that Carrie had thought I'd meant that Erin was *gone*—as in stuffed a suitcase and left me.

Carrie said, "Greg, I think you two need to come over to our house tonight. Gary and I have been meaning to talk to you for a long time."

Apparently our marriage issues were obvious enough to have

caused the Olivers distress and concern about the stability of our relationship. I was embarrassed but also relieved. I loved and respected the Olivers, and their marriage was what I wanted ours to be like.

We all four met in their living room, and the Olivers began to mentor Erin and me in how to love each another. For the first time Erin and I had a couple to talk to, to share our problems with in a real, honest, and straightforward manner.

If your marriage is strong, even if all the circumstances in your life . . . are filled with trouble and weakness, it won't matter. You will be able to move out into the world in strength.

Timothy Keller, *The Meaning of Marriage*

Over three years, Erin and I watched them as carefully as movie critic evaluates a film. Each day the Olivers gave us a new take on life, a new scene from which to gather insight. We not only learned about marriage and how to have an intimate, spiritual relationship, but we also learned about parenting and how to be coworkers. Their example created a dream for us: we began believing we could get along well enough to speak at marriage events together and to counsel other couples together.

I also met alone with Gary. We jogged together, and he would tell me just what it meant to be a husband. He was always a good listener, but he would never tolerate my griping about Erin. Instead he would recommend ways for *me* to change, saying things like, "Here's the attitude you need to have when you interact with Erin." Over the decades, he has consistently prayed for me and has texted, emailed, and phoned me with encouragement.

The Olivers' calling was to pour into us, and when Carrie was diagnosed with cancer, Erin and I had a chance to pour into them—to give back. We encouraged them, brought them meals, prayed for and with them, and after Carrie died, we supported Gary as he mourned.

A mentor couple fills a role similar to the role the apostle Paul brought to the early church. He provided insight, wisdom, and acted as an inspiration to others. He was a shepherd to the members of several new churches.[4] Erin and I call mentor couples "Paul Couples" for that reason.

A mentor couple is typically an older, experienced husband and wife who can offer great wisdom because they have already walked the same road as a younger couple. The older couple provides mentorship and invests in the younger couple's relationship through faithful prayer and godly advice.

2. Peer Encouragers

When Erin and I lived in La Mirada, California, I was attending the Rosemead School of Psychology at Biola University. Taylor was an infant. Erin was working as a nurse, picking up night shifts. Erin recalls our peer encouragers:

> We had two couples who were our friends during the
> Rosemead years. They were my lifeline. Because I worked

night shifts, I had a lopsided schedule, but they still made the effort to hang out with us. It wasn't a formalized small group, but they were a salve that Greg and I needed. We could actually enjoy time with each other when we were with these friends. During this time, our marriage didn't improve much, but it was at least stabilized somewhat by the influence of our friends.

One couple, Alisa and Chris Grace, had two kids, providing Taylor with playmates close to her age. Alisa especially supported and validated me as mom. Being with her reinforced in my heart that I did have something to offer as a mother and as a wife.

The second couple, Chip and Rebecca Dickens didn't have kids when we met, but we were friends with them during the pregnancy of their first child. I also had the honor of being their assistant nurse when baby Josh was born. That was one way in which I hope they were encouraged by my friendship; I felt as if I was giving rather than always taking. They were "behind" us on the baby thing, but Chip was already an undergraduate professor, and we saw how well he and Rebecca supported each other.

The Graces and the Dickenses were a sounding board for us. We were on a life journey together. We watched them interact and learned that not all couples argued like we did. Alisa, especially, was a good example. Chris is a funny guy like Greg. But she has a more tenderhearted and calm spirit than I do. By watching her, I learned that it was possible not to be so reactive and critical.

The peer couples whom you cultivate as friends should be in the same season of life. They usually have been married roughly the same number of years and/or have children of similar ages. Erin and I call peer couples "Barnabas Couples" on life's journey. These couples offer regular encouragement and friendship, such as Barnabas did for the apostle Paul and the early church.[5]

3. Younger Friends or Couples

For more than a decade, I've invested in the life of a friend named Jackson Dunn. I met Jackson at John Brown University.

> *[Spiritual leadership is] knowing where God wants people to be and taking the initiative to use God's methods to get them there in reliance on God's power.*
>
> John Piper, *Desiring God*

Let me tell you one reason Jackson is the right type to be my mentee: he can appreciate a good prank. The first time he went hiking with me and the kids, he passed the Smalley "can you take a joke?" test. On this warm and humid summer day, we planned to take my Ford Explorer Sport Trac into the hills. The kids—Taylor, Murphy, and Garrison—graciously offered Jackson the coveted front passenger seat, but before Jackson sat down, I tripped the seat-warmer button, which is tucked way under the seat, hiding the telltale glow that it's been turned on.

As we drove along the highway and chatted, I would occasionally glance at Jackson. I *almost* felt sorry for him. It was morning, and he had the east-facing window, which left him open to the blaring sun. He was dressed in black too, so his clothes were absorbing heat. Sweat dribbled down his temples, and he was wiping it off with his sleeve. He would constantly put his hand on the air vent, checking to make sure the AC hadn't gone off. In the back seat, the kids were giggling, barely able to ward off all-out guffaws.

*Some day you will find out that there
is far more happiness in another's
happiness than in your own.*

Honoré de Balzac, *Père Goriot*

After we stopped at the trailhead and parked, Jackson quickly hopped out of the car. By then we Smalleys couldn't hide our secret any longer.

"Did you notice you're the only one sweating?" I asked.

Curious, Jackson glanced at each of our faces. "Yeah," he said, "it was hot in there even though the air conditioner was going."

As the kids burst into laughter, I showed him the button and confessed the secret. He smiled and politely laughed, revealing the unflappable class and graciousness that are hallmarks of his character.

Since that day, Jackson and I have done ministry together. We're bonded by a common cause, to fight for biblical marriage in a hedonistic culture. He and I worked at the Center for

Healthy Relationships under Gary Oliver. And in 2011 when I joined the staff at Focus on the Family, he came to Focus with me as the director of the marriage department.

Over the years, Jackson and his wife Krista have become some of our closest friends and our families have many shared memories.

Hiking with Jackson, working alongside him, praying with him, worshiping with him, watching him parent, leaning on him—I'm sure I've grown more through our relationship than he has.

Recently, Jackson left his position as my right-hand man. I am torn. In one respect I know God is leading him to a new workplace where Jackson's talents and gift will be developed. But for now, our day-to-day friendship is over, and I'll miss him. Our fellowship, however, will remain strong because we have a shared vision, one that Jackson will carry with him throughout his life.

It's amazing how much *you* will receive when you mentor a younger person or couple. Jackson isn't my only mentee. Erin and I have reached out to other individuals and couples at our marriage seminars, and we've grown closer as a result. If you and your spouse work as a team to help others, you'll become much more relationally aware, improve your own communication skills, and grow closer to each other. Your marriage will become stronger as you reach outward in fellowship.

These younger friends are individuals or couples who are at least five years younger, perhaps even an engaged couple who are looking for mentorship. This type of mentor-mentee relationship is defined in Titus 2:3-5. Older women are to "teach what is good. Then they can train the younger women to love their husbands and children, to be self-controlled and pure, to be busy at home, to be kind, and to be subject to their husbands, so that no one will malign the word of God." There's no reason that men shouldn't likewise teach younger guys how to love their wives, raise godly children, and live the Christian life.

FELLOWSHIP OF THE CHURCH

I'm an introvert, so when Erin suggests I go with her to parties or dinners, I go only because I want to share the experience with her. But when an opportunity arises to join a group of other likeminded couples who want to support our marriage, I'm all in.

Couple friends can offer much-needed spiritual support during difficult times as well as in our times of celebration. This biblical model is described in Proverbs 17:17: "A friend loves at all times, and a brother is born for adversity." Close friends give each other the encouragement needed to keep going, as well as a shoulder to cry on, or what I need sometimes—a kick in the proverbial pants.

> When we display our best selves for friends, at the same time we draw closer.

I find that when Erin and I are close to other couples, we are often on our best behavior. We find ourselves more engaged in conversation, sharing stories from our past, describing why we found each other to be attractive in the first place. When we display our best selves for friends, at the same time we draw closer, rekindling those early, passionate feelings of admiration and attraction.

Ever since we got married, Erin has found friendship and support through structured Bible studies led by married women. "I was new to discipleship. I loved going to Bible studies where the women would affirm me and teach me spiritual principles. Those women and those studies kept me going. I learned that God created me to have strengths; I was valuable."

TRANSPARENCY IS KEY TO FELLOWSHIP

Remember, there is one fundamental key to experiencing the many benefits of sharing your marriage journey with others, of having community. It depends on your willingness to self-disclose—becoming vulnerable by revealing your deepest thoughts, fears, beliefs, feelings, dreams, goals, failures, and struggles.

The apostle Paul cared for the church community in Thessolonica so much that he wrote, "We loved you so much that we were delighted to share with you not only the gospel of God but our lives as well" (1 Thessalonians 2:8).

Isn't being real worth the risk of being discovered—found out as flawed and human, just like everybody else? Yet all too often, we are threatened by the thought of being honest about our inner lives and our personal challenges. We have trouble living out James 5:16, and confessing our sins. We choose to hold up a smiling mask and try to convey that everything in our world is just fine, thank you. Why is it hard to be transparent when the rewards are so clear?

What makes it difficult for many of us to be transparent?

For some, the fear of not being accepted is paralyzing. Experiences going back to early childhood can leave scars that prevent the trust necessary for full and open disclosure.

Often the issue is real-life demands of children or aging parents—or both—on our time and energy, leaving little space for transparent relationships. A draining job or a financial struggle might take away the motivation and drive of one or both partners in a marriage, causing them to switch into survival mode and focus on the home front only.

Personalities weigh into the issue of developing relationships

---

BOUNDARIES IN YOUR FRIENDSHIPS

For those navigating opposite-gender friendships with married friends, Suzanne Hadley Gosselin, a blogger for Focus on the Family's Boundless website, offers two principles:

1. Have a friendship that is above reproach. If your spouse and/or others think it seems fishy, it probably is.
2. Honor the couple above the friendship. This may mean modifying the level of friendship you have had in the past for the good of your friend's marital relationship.

Suzanne also notes,

I have appreciated how my husband, Kevin, has welcomed my male friends as "our" friends. I don't do things with male friends alone, but instead my husband and I extend friendship to them together. Plus, if Kevin even has a hint of uneasiness with a particular friendship, I respect his wishes on the matter."[6]

as well. While some seek the thrill of connection, others find it a struggle to maintain multiple relationships and prefer time alone in order to recharge. Yet sometimes the best networkers are more comfortable with superficial relationships, while classic introverts can share deeply with a few people in their lives. Each individual has his or her own experience with transparency, and it is more difficult for some than others.

> *Answering God's call as a couple can bring new life to a marriage relationship.*

Regardless of how both members of a couple are wired as individuals, Christians are called to reach out to help others—to encourage one another daily (Hebrews 3:13). Answering God's call as a couple can bring new life to a marriage relationship, in spite of challenges.

WHERE AND HOW TO CONNECT IN YOUR COMMUNITY

Look around in your own world to discover the calling and connections God may have for you today.

If you think about your world as a series of concentric circles, you'll discover a wealth of opportunities for building relationships together:

• Start with your neighborhood and local schools if your children are attending there. Consider how you can meet your neighbors and share life with them regularly. Look for even the most basic connecting points such as book clubs and volunteer activities.

- Your church likely offers multiple opportunities to connect with people of all ages and discover the divine appointments God has already set for you.
- Workplace relationships form a natural bridge to building trust and growing closer to others—those who share a similar background and those who may be very different from you.
- If you have a specific, shared passion, seek out regional volunteer activities and discover the broader world of relationships your community provides.
- Finally, consider opportunities to get involved with others nationally and internationally through global outreach such as mission trips, worthy causes, and healthy social media activities.

TWENTY-ONE WAYS TO INVEST IN ANOTHER COUPLE'S MARRIAGE

As we noted, meeting regularly with another couple in a mentoring relationship is a great way to invest in building marriages. But there are a host of other ways you can encourage couples around you as well. Some involve simple gestures, others will require a little effort. Scan the following list for creative ideas about how you and your spouse can help build stronger marriages in your church, neighborhood, and community.

1. Organize a progressive dinner for couples on your street.
2. Meet with an engaged couple to go through a marriage preparation book together.

3. You and your spouse bring dessert, flowers, or a small care package to welcome a new couple into the neighborhood.

4. Start a couples' book club.

5. Invite another couple on a double-date with you, seasoning your time together with marriage-building conversation.

6. Volunteer to lead a Sunday school class for young married couples.

7. Invite a couple that doesn't attend church to attend with you.

8. Invite another couple to attend an upcoming marriage conference with you.

9. Mentor a less-experienced couple by meeting once a month for the next year.

10. Offer to babysit for a cash-strapped couple with young children so they can enjoy an evening out by themselves.

11. If you're aware of another couple's anniversary, send them a card and maybe a small gift to celebrate the occasion.

12. Form friendships with other spouses of your gender in your neighborhood and encourage them in their marriages. Share some tea or coffee or invite the person to a fun outing. Offer a safe haven, a listening ear, and a reassuring voice.

13. Organize an event at your church to honor couples who have reached fifty years or another significant milestone, and give them an opportunity to share their stories and lessons learned.

14. Pay for an online relationship assessment for a couple considering marriage.
15. Spearhead a marriage mentoring ministry at your church (with your pastor's blessing), perhaps pairing each newly married couple with a more experienced one.
16. Give a marriage devotional book as a Christmas present.
17. Host an engagement party to celebrate the event for a couple who has taken that step toward marriage.
18. Help organize a Valentine's Day celebration at your church.
19. Be spontaneous! Invite another couple for an impromptu backyard barbecue or to join you at the movies that evening.
20. Trade houses with another couple for a weekend as a cheap get-away.
21. Look for opportunities to compliment couples you know for the way they demonstrate love for one another.

We all have a responsibility to help build a community of support and encouragement for our own marriages and for other couples as well. Never forget, "Marriage should be honored by all" (Hebrews 13:4). Start by setting aside special time together to brainstorm your own ideas as a couple about where you can best begin.

Help One Another Through the Fiery Trials

Music artist Plumb, aka Tiffany Arbuckle Lee, tells how Christian fellowship helped hold her marriage together after Jeremy, her husband, sent her a text message saying he was leaving—and her world went black.

> The only true thing of beauty during this winter was how our community held us up. All those friends who had been with us since our dating days, rallied around us . . . Two days after [Jeremy] left me, forty of our closest friends gathered in the chapel we were married in to pray for us. They held us up in prayer, then in the following weeks and months ahead held us up physically with calls, food, babysitting, and more prayers.[7]

The next time you're at a wedding, remember the Council of Elrond. The couple who is getting married is going to face hardships, and like Tiffany and Jeremy Lee, they may need your help if their marriage is facing death. Join the couple's "fellowship of the wedding rings" when the person officiating asks, and say, "We do."

Remember to visit *crazylittlethingcalledmarriage.com* to find the bonus material: the marriage assessment, the twelve date night ideas, and the discussion questions.

THE
PROMISED LAND
OF MARRIAGE

As this book draws to a close, you've now explored twelve traits, or habits, of a thriving marriage. You've learned a lot about how to make a marriage successful, and you've seen how to put those habits into daily practice.

The goal is to enjoy what we might call a Promised Land Marriage—a place, or relationship, "flowing with milk and honey" (Exodus 3:8), where you experience all God intended marriage to be. That's really possible, as countless joyfully married couples can attest.

But like the ancient Israelites when they took up residence in their Promised Land, I can get off track. And I think you may get off track sometimes too. It's so easy to get distracted from your daily purpose of building a thriving marriage. You can be influenced by the surrounding culture, which encourages you to walk away from marriage when the going gets tough or you're just not happy anymore. You can grow reliant on your own abilities rather than recognizing your dependence on God's strength and wisdom.

Like the Israelites who lived in their Promised Land for a number of years and forgot about God's goodness, we all need to be reminded of the commitment we've made to God and, in our case, to our spouse.

> We need to choose, every day, to pursue a great marriage.

Just as Joshua challenged his people to "choose this day whom you will serve" (Joshua 24:15, ESV), so we need to choose, every day, to pursue a great marriage.

We need to choose intentionality over passivity . . .

Loving thoughts over self-centered thoughts . . .

Loving actions over self-serving ones.

And in the process of keeping your commitments and acting in love, you will find yourselves enjoying true Promised Land Marriage. Which brings me back to Erin and that Hawaiian waterfall where we had the first big fight of our marriage.

Many people will tell you to focus on your marriage, to focus on each other; but we discovered that focusing on God's mission made our marriage amazing.

Francis Chan, *You and Me Forever*

I realized we had entered our promised land when we led a marriage seminar on the same Hawaiian island where we had honeymooned—the one that had the beautiful waterfall I didn't get to enjoy.

Erin and I had now been married for about fifteen years, so it had been a long time since I'd been on the island. After the seminar was over, she surprised me with a rain forest hike. We had been walking for about an hour when we came upon a waterfall with a beautiful pool at the bottom.

I stood there with my mouth open wide in shock. It was the same waterfall where we had our first major conflict but the sign was gone. Somehow, I hadn't recognized the area where we'd been hiking.

The biggest surprise was that this time, Erin jumped right into the pool without hesitation—she didn't even wait for me! She swam over to the waterfall, climbed up to a rock outcropping about twenty feet in the air, and jumped back into the pool. I was awestruck.

"Are you just going to stand there," she playfully shouted, "or are we going to jump together?"

Although it took nearly fifteen years, we had definitely come full circle. Just as the ancient Israelites had needed to get past the massive walls of Jericho to enter their promised land, I guess we needed to get past a waterfall.

Erin jumped right into the pool without hesitation.

Now what about you? Are you ready to enjoy a Promised Land Marriage? Are you willing to do the work, knowing that with God's help you can also reap the rewards? Make that choice, make that commitment, today and every day. If you do, this crazy little thing called marriage will become both your greatest service to Him and your greatest source of true and lasting joy.

Acknowledgments

Erin and I would like to thank the many people who supported us in writing *Crazy Little Thing Called Marriage*.

First and foremost, Marianne Hering, you are an amazing writer! There are no words for your contribution. Although we know that this was an assignment you accepted, your effort, commitment, and love for both Erin and me went above and beyond. Your commitment to excellence speaks volumes about your character. You have truly been a joy to work with and we look forward to the next project we get to share—that is if you would graciously accept another one!

We'd like to share our deep gratitude to the marriage team at Focus on the Family. Your daily support, love, and encouragement, both now and over the past five years, has been priceless. On those days that are challenging, it is always one of you who offers just the right words or makes us laugh when it is needed most. Thank you to the Family Ministries team at Focus: Jackson Dunn, Heather Dedrick, Sarah Mason, Karen Reedall, Treshia Kuiper, Nina Coppola, Hannah Fessler, Lisa Anderson, and Anthony Ashley. Also, thank you to Edie Nielsen, Pam Woody, and Brian Neils. You are irreplaceable!

This book would not have been possible without the hard work of both the Focus on the Family editorial team—Larry Weeden, Liz Duckworth, and Angela Messinger—and also the Tyndale team. Thank you for your vision and work to bring this book into fruition.

Thank you to Jim Daly and Ken Windebank for your leadership at Focus on the Family and your commitment to strengthening marriages. Your continued efforts do not go unnoticed. We are honored to be part of your team at Focus and count it a privilege to serve alongside of you both in marriage ministry. Truly you are wonderful men of God, and you love our staff at Focus so well.

Thank you to the pioneers in the Christian marriage world such as John Gottman, Scott Stanley, Gary Oliver, and our dad, Gary Smalley—who continue to study and learn more about what makes marriages succeed. Also, thank you to the National Institute of Marriage team. We could not do what we do without your continued research and investigation of understanding how to help couples.

Last, thank you to our four wonderful children—Taylor, Murphy, Garrison, and Annie. You are each such a blessing in your own right—Taylor, your gentle spirit; Murphy, your strength and compassion; Garrison, your love for people and, oh yes, college football; and Annie, your spark and spunk for life. God has blessed us more than you will ever know by allowing us to be your mom and dad. Thank you for loving us in return and allowing us to be human as we parent you through all the different stages of life. We love you dearly!

To Greg—I love you more than words can express. Your continual efforts to improve both personally and professionally are a gift. Your commitment to your family—even in the craziness of life—speak volumes to the man that you are. Thank you for loving us so well! We love you more than you can imagine!

To Erin—You are an amazing wife and mother. God has

truly gifted you as a counselor, speaker, and writer. I'm thrilled to partner with you to strengthen marriages around the world. Thank you for being my best friend and for the ongoing support and encouragement. I love you!

Erin Smalley

Notes

This Thing Called Love

1. Drew DeSilver, "5 Facts About Love and Marriage," Pew Research Center: FactTank, February 14, 2014, http://www.pewresearch.org /fact-tank/2014/02/14/5-facts-about-love-and-marriage/.
2. Susan Ratcliffe, ed., *Concise Oxford Dictionary of Quotations,* s.v. George Sand: letter to Lina Calamatta, March 31, 1862, 315, https://books.google.com/books?id=KRiFmlT2cdIC&pg=PA315 &dq=george+sand+there+is+only+one+happiness+in+life+let ter+1862+oxford+dictionary+of+quotes&hl=en&sa=X&ved =0CB4Q6AEwAGoVChMIvM-K4biSxgIVUpqICh3uMwD H#v=onepage&q=george%20sand%20there%20is%20only%20 one%20happiness%20in%20life%20letter%201862%20 oxford%20dictionary%20of%20quotes&f=false.
3. "Somebody To Love You," *Revelations*, MCA Nashville, 1996. Lyrics by Gary Nicholson and Delbert McClinton. Copyright: Lew-bob Songs.
4. *The Free Dictionary*, s.v. sacrifice.

Romance Secret #1: True Love Commits

1. *Merriam-Webster Online,* s.v. wholehearted.
2. Sun Tzu, translated by Lionel Giles, *The Art of War: Illustrated Edition* (New York: Fall River Press, 2014), 72.
3. Tu Yu, quoted in *The Art of War*, 221.
4. Tu Mu, quoted in *The Art of War*, 196.
5. This man's name has several spellings, and his history is obscure, most often noted in books written in foreign languages about the history of Islam or Spain. *Wikipedia* has the best reference to the "burn the boats" event that I could understand without first obtaining a master's degree in Spanish or Islamic history. For more information see the *Wiki* entry for "Tariq ibn Ziyad" at https:// wikipedia.org/wiki/Tariq_ibn_Ziyad.
6. *Sparknotes,* "The Aeneid: Book V," accessed July 1, 2015, http:// www.sparknotes.com/lit/aeneid/section5.rhtml.

7. Several leadership books recount Alexander the Great saying, "We go home in Persian boats, or we die!" However, I was unable to document this incident in any reputable history book.

8. Aztec-History.com, "Aztec Warriors," accessed July 1, 2015, http://www.aztec-history.com/aztec-warriors.html.

9. Never one to let a few facts ruin a great story, I use this oft-told legend because it's vivid and dramatic. Do an Internet search for "images Cortés burning" to see some glorious paintings of Cortés's burning ships. However, if you're a stickler for accuracy, I have to tell you that modern historians assert that while Cortés did dismantle his ships, he didn't actually burn them.

10. Scott Stanley, "The Half-Hearted Marriage," accessed July 3, 2015, http://www.focusonthefamily.com/marriage/strengthening-your -marriage/commitment/the-half-hearted-marriage, originally published in *Focus on the Family* magazine, January 2007, © Scott Stanley.

11. American Psychological Association, "Religion or Spirituality Has Positive Impact on Romantic/Marital Relationships, Child Development, Research Shows," news release, December 12, 2014, http://www.apa.org/news/press/releases/2014/12/religion -relationships.aspx.

12. Stanley, "The Half-Hearted Marriage," Focus on the Family magazine.

Romance Secret #2: True Love Seeks God

1. Sun Tzu, translated by Lionel Giles, *The Art of War: Illustrated Edition* (New York: Fall River Press, 2014), 78.

2. Ibid., 79.

3. Christopher Ellison, "The Religion of Couples, Relationship Quality, and Health," *UTSA (University of Texas at San Antonio) Discovery*, 4 (2011), https://www.utsa.edu/discovery/2011/story /feature-religion.html.

4. Alfred DeMaris, Katherine G. Kusner, Annette Mahoney, and Kenneth I. Pargament, "Sanctification of Marriage and Spiritual Intimacy Predicting Observed Marital Interactions Across the Transition to Parenthood," *Journal of Family Psychology*, 28, no. 5, (2014): 611, http://www.apa.org/pubs/journals/releases/fam-a0036989.pdf.

5. Jakob F. Jensen, Allen K. Sabey, and Amy J. Rauer, "Compassionate Love as a Mechanism Linking Sacred Qualities of Marriage to Older Couples' Marital Satisfaction," *Journal of Family Psychology*, 28, no. 5 (2014), 594, http://www.apa.org/pubs/journals/releases/fam-a0036991.pdf.

6. Solomon's Temple was destroyed in the sixth-century BC. The second temple was destroyed in 70. Many Bible scholars estimate that the apostle Paul wrote the letter to the Ephesians circa 62.

7. Paul Trebilco, *The Early Christians in Ephesus from Paul to Ignatius*, (Grand Rapids, MI: Eerdmans, 2007), 20.

8. Cited by Georgia State University Department of Physics and Astronomy, "Nuclear Fission," *HyperPhysics,* accessed September 22, 2015, http://hyperphysics.phy-astr.gsu.edu/hbase/nucene/fission.html.

9. Statistic based on an interview with Sequoia National Park representative, September 30, 2015. The park receives more than two million visitors per year.

10. News Release Today, "Gary Smalley Author Profile," news release, accessed July 25, 2015, http://www.newreleasetoday.com/author detail.php?aut_id=21.

11. Robertson McQuilkin, *A Promise Kept* (Carol Stream, IL: Tyndale, 1998), 6-7.

12. Ibid, 21-23.

13. See Acts 18:2, 18:18-19, 18:26; Romans 16:3; 1 Corinthians 16:19; 2 Timothy 4:19.

14. US Environmental Protection Agency, "Clean Energy: Nuclear Power," accessed August 22, 2015, http://www.epa.gov/cleanenergy/energy-and-you/affect/nuclear.html.

15. Jonathan Cobb, "How Many Homes Can the Typical Nuclear Power Plant Power?," Answers.com, accessed August 22, 2015, http://www.answers.com/Q/How_many_homes_can_the_typical_nuclear_power_plant_power.

16. Lisa Zyga, "Mini Nuclear Power Plants Could Power 20,000 Homes," Phys.Org, November 12, 2008, http://phys.org/news/2008-11-mini-nuclear-power-homes.html.

17. *Dictionary.com*, s.v. synergy.

18. Neil Clark Warren, *The Triumphant Marriage* (Nashville: Thomas Nelson, 1995), 18.
19. *A Promise Kept*, 18-19.

Romance Secret #3: True Love Strives to Know and Be Known

1. Rochelle Bilow, "Want Your Marriage to Last?" *Your Tango*, November 18, 2013, http://www.yourtango.com/experts/rochelle -bilow/want-your-marriage-last?utm_source=huffingtonpost.com &utm_medium=referral&utm_campaign=pubexchange_article.
2. That number does not include the crown jewel of fan fiction: *Pride and Prejudice and Zombies*. IMDB, "Pride and Prejudice," accessed August 5, 2015, http://www.imdb.com/find?q=pride+and+prejudic e&s=tt&ref_=fn_al_tt_mr.
3. Amy Bellows, "Good Communication in Marriage Starts with Respect," Psych Central, January 30, 2013, http://psychcentral .com/lib/good-communication-in-marriage-starts-with-respect/.
4. Your Tango Experts, "5 Ways Men & Women Communicate Differently," *Psych Central*, last updated July 16, 2014, http:// psychcentral.com/blog/archives/2012/04/01/6-ways-men-and -women-communicate-differently/.
5. Tonya Reiman, "Gender Differences in Communication," Body Language University, accessed August 7, 2015, http://www.body languageuniversity.com/public/213.cfm.
6. Julie Huynh, "Study Finds No Difference in the Amount Men and Women Talk," Undergraduate Biology Research Program: University of Arizona, June 19, 2014, https://ubrp.arizona.edu/study -finds-no-difference-in-the-amount-men-and-women-talk/.
7. Ibid.
8. Audrey Nelson, "Why You Stand Side-by-Side or Face-to-Face," *Psychology Today* (blog), April 27, 2014, https://www.psychology today.com/blog/he-speaks-she-speaks/201404/why-you-stand-side -side-or-face-face.
9. Zheng Yan, ed., *Encyclopedia of Mobile Phone Use* (Hershey, PA: Information Science Reference, 2015), 781.
10. Tasuku Igarashi, Jiro Takai, and Toshikazu Yoshida, "Gender Differences in Social Network Development via Mobile Phone Text

Messages: A Longitudinal Study," Journal of Social and Personal Relationships October 2005, 22: abstract.

11. *Encyclopedia of Mobile Phone Use,* 324.

12. Ibid., 327.

13. Diogenes Laërtius, *Delphi Complete Works of Diogenes Laërtius* (Delphi Classics, 2015), Zeno.

14. Scott Williams, "Listening Effectively," Wright State University, accessed August 9, 2015, http://www.wright.edu/~scott.williams /skills/listening.htm.

15. Though this quote has been attributed to eighteenth-century German statesman Johann Wolfgang von Goethe, the source could not be verified. But whoever did say it first was right on the money!

Romance Secret #4: True Love Fights for Peace

1. Scott M. Stanley, Howard J. Markman, Michelle St. Peters and B. Douglas Leber (Oct., 1995). Strengthening Marriages and Preventing Divorce: New Directions in Prevention Research, *Family Relations*, Vol. 44, No. 4, pp. 392-401.

2. "*Batman v Superman: Dawn of Justice*—Comic-Con Trailer [HD]" YouTube, minute 2:36, accessed September 27, 2015, https://www .youtube.com/watch?v=0WWzgGyAH6Y.

3. B. R. Karney and L. A. Neff, "Stress and reactivity to daily relationship experiences: How stress hinders adaptive processes in marriage," *Journal of Personality and Social Psychology*, 97 no. 3 (September 2009), 435-450.

4. 1 Corinthians 1:10

5. John 8:44

6. 1 Corinthians 13:4-5

7. Proverbs 15:1

Romance Secret #5: True Love Honors

1. YouTube, *The Run List Channel,* uploaded July 11, 2013, https:// www.youtube.com/watch?v=kiLxdQEWYIg.

2. Adapted from Greg Smalley, *Fight Your Way to a Better Marriage*, (New York: Howard, 2012), 165-167.

3. John Gottman and Nan Silver, *The Seven Principles for Making Marriage Work* (New York: Harmony, 1999, 2015), 71.

4. *Strong's Concordance*, s.v. 5902 *timē*, http://biblehub.com/greek
   /5092.htm.
5. Boaz refers to people as being younger than he is. See Ruth 2:8,
   2:5, 3:10. There were several self-published commentaries that
   agreed with this age estimate, but not many of the true scholarly
   works would cite a specific age, leaving preachers like me no choice
   but to take the text at face value.
6. Deuteronomy 24:19, Leviticus 19:9, Leviticus 23:22.
7. Boaz gave them an *ephah* of barley, which is a bushel in today's
   farming lingo. A bushel of barley is forty-eight pounds, according
   the US Administrative Codes, http://www.ilga.gov/commission
   /jcar/admincode/008/00800600ZZ9998bR.html. I did the math.
   If Naomi and Ruth ate barley for three meals a day at a normal
   serving (157 grams), the forty-eight pounds (21772.4 grams)
   would last the two women twenty-three days.
8. *Matthew Henry's Concise Commentary*, s.v. Ruth 3:6-13, http://
   biblehub.com/commentaries/ruth/3-10.htm.
9. *Strong's Concordance*, s.v. 632 *aponemó*, http://biblehub.com
   /greek/632.htm.
10. Food Editorial.Co, "What Makes the Starbucks Coffee Experience
    Special?," accessed October 13, 2015, http://www.streetdirectory
    .com/food_editorials/beverages/coffee/what_makes_the_starbucks
    _coffee_experience_special.html.
11. *GB Times*, "Woman Files for Divorce After Groom Gets Her
    Name Wrong," July 08, 2013, http://gbtimes.com/china
    /woman-files-divorce-after-groom-gets-her-name-wrong
    -wedding.

Romance Secret #6: True Love Nourishes

1. National Institute of Diabetes, Digestive, and Kidney Diseases,
   "Overweight and Obesity Statistics," accessed July 21, 2015, http://
   www.niddk.nih.gov/health-information/health-statistics/Pages
   /overweight-obesity-statistics.aspx.
2. *Strong's Concordance*, s.v. 1625 *ektrephó*.
3. See also Leviticus 26:4, Deuteronomy 28:12 and 32:2, 2 Samuel
   23:4, 1 Kings 8:36, Job 5:10, and 2 Chronicles 6:27.
4. Young's Literal Translation, public domain.

5. *Dictionary.com*, s.v. servant.
6. John Ortberg, *The Life You've Always Wanted* (Grand Rapids: Zondervan, 2009), 105.
7. Jennifer Duke, "Pride and Prejudice Still on Top," *Upstart*, June 10, 2010, http://www.upstart.net.au/2010/06/10/pride-and-prejudice-still-on-top/.
8. The National Healthy Marriage Institute, "Samples," accessed October 1, 2015, http://www.healthymarriage.org/marriage tipssamples.htm.
9. Captain Frank Crescitelli, quoted in Monte Burke, "Leadership Lessons from Fishing Guides," *Forbes*, May 24, 2012, http://www.forbes.com/sites/monteburke/2012/05/24/leadership-lessons-from-fishing-guides/2/.
10. This list was augmented from Marriage Missions International, "100 Ways You Can Love Your Husband HIS Way," accessed October 10, 2015, http://marriagemissions.com/100-ways-you-can-love-your-husband-his-way/.
11. Augmented and adapted from Marriage Missions International, "100 Ways You Can Love Your Wife HER Way," accessed October 10, 2015, http://marriagemissions.com/100-ways-you-can-love-your-wife-her-way/.

Romance Secret #7: True Love Needs Time to Grow

1. William F. Harley Jr., *His Needs, Her Needs: Building An Affair-Proof Marriage* (Grand Rapids: Revell, 2011), 70.
2. M. Gary Neuman, "New Year's Resolutions for Your Marriage," *Huffington Post* (blog), December 31, 2012, http://www.huffington post.com/m-gary-neuman/new-years-resolutions-for_b_2389532 .html; and Dana Fillmore, "Dr. Dana's Help if You Have Grown Apart from Your Spouse," Strong Marriage Now, accessed October 7, 2011, https://www.strongmarriagenow.com/important-problem /grown-apart-yt/.
3. Ibid., Fillmore.
4. W. Bradford Wilcox and Jeffrey Dew, *The Date Night Opportunity: What Does Couple Time Tell Us about the Potential Value of Date Nights?* (Charlottesville, VA: National Marriage Project/University of Virginia, 2012), 5.

5. David Mace, quoted in John R. Buri, *How to Love Your Wife* (Mustang, OK: Tate Publishing, 2006), 57.

6. Leslie Becker-Phelps, "Time Together: A Cure for Relationship Problems," April 27, 2011, WebMD (blog), http://blogs.webmd .com/art-of-relationships/2011/04/time-together-a-cure-for -relationship-problems.html.

7. IMDb, "Mrs. Doubtfire (1993): Quotes," accessed October 3, 2015, http://www.imdb.com/title/tt0107614/quotes.

8. Roy Croft, quoted in Hazel Felleman (ed.), *Best Loved Poems of the American People* (New York: Doubleday, 1936), 25.

9. Carolyn Pirak, "Make Time for Your Partner," ParentMap (blog), August 26, 2008, https://www.parentmap.com/article/make-time -for-your-partner.

10. Michele Weiner-Davis, "Time Together," Divorce Busting: Michele's Articles, © 2009, accessed October 7, 2015, http://www .divorcebusting.com/a_time_together.htm.

11. Dana Fillmore, "Dr. Dana's Help if You Have Grown Apart from Your Spouse," Strong Marriage Now, accessed October 7, 2011, https://www.strongmarriagenow.com/important-problem/grown -apart-yt/.

12. Becker-Phelps, "Time Together: A Cure for Relationship Problems."

13. Lois Clark, "Building a Strong Marriage: Finding Time," The Ohio State University Extension: Family Life Month Packet 2002, 2, http://ohioline.osu.edu/flm02/pdf/fs02.pdf.

14. Pirak, "Make Time for Your Partner."

15. Wilcox and Dew, *The Date Night Opportunity*, 6.

16. Tara Parker Pope, "Reinventing Date Night for Long-Married Couples," *New York Times*, February 12, 2008, http://www .nytimes.com/2008/02/12/health/12well.html?_r=0.

17. Ibid.

18. Arthur Szabo, *Selecta* (a West German science magazine circa 1968), quoted in Margaret Anderson Bonn, "Morning Kiss Really Counts," *The Virgin Islands Daily News*, June 26, 1968, 10, 13, quoted in Noelia Trujillo, "10 Oh-So Fascinating Facts About Kissing," *Good Housekeeping*, March 16, 2015, http://www.goodhousekeeping .com/life/relationships/advice/a31659/kissing-facts/.

Romance Secret #8: True Love Embraces

1. Mark Driscoll, "What the Bible Really Says About Sex," January 3, 2012, *Fox News Opinion* (blog), http://www.foxnews.com /opinion/2012/01/03/what-bible-really-says-about-sex/.

2. Rochelle Peachy, quoted in Diana Appleyard, "How Important Is Sex to a Marriage?," Daily Mail, June 23, 2011, http://www.dailymail .co.uk/femail/article-2007065/How-important-sex-marriage -Passion-marriage-wane-So-YOU-making-priority.html.

3. Francine Kaye, quoted in Diana Appleyard, "How Important Is Sex to a Marriage."

4. Al Mohler, "The Meaning of Sex in Marriage," Crosswalk.com (blog), June 3, 2008, http://www.crosswalk.com/family/marriage /the-meaning-of-sex-in-marriage-1335493.html.

5. Donald Paglia, "Sex and Intimacy: The Marital Sexual Relation-ship," accessed October 16, 2015, For Your Marriage.org (blog), https://www.foryourmarriage.org/the-marital-sexual-relationship/

6. Juli Slattery, *No More Headaches* (Carol Stream, IL: Tyndale, Focus on the Family, 2009), 107.

7. Donald Paglia, "Sex and Intimacy: The Marital Sexual Relationship."

8. Adapted from Erin Smalley, Greg Smalley, and Gary Smalley, *The Wholehearted Wife* (Carol Stream, IL: Tyndale, Focus on the Family, 2014), 117-118, 135-136.

9. Dr. Kevin Leman, *Sheet Music* (Carol Stream, IL: Tyndale House Publishers, 2008), 215.

10. Mandy Kirby, "First World War: Love Letters from the Trenches," *The Telegraph*, January 15, 2014, http://www.telegraph.co.uk /history/world-war-one/10561261/First-World-War-love-letters -from-the-trenches.html.

11. John Eldredge and Stasi Eldredge, *Love and War: Find Your Way to Something Beautiful in Your Marriage* (Colorado Springs, CO: WaterBrook, 2011), 175.

Romance Secret #9: True Love Serves

1. *Everybody Loves Raymond*, Season 7, Episode 22, "Baggage."

2. Pew Research Center, "Modern Marriage," July 18, 2007, http:// www.pewsocialtrends.org/2007/07/18/modern-marriage/.

3. Ibid.

4. Virginia Rutler, "Love and Lust," *Psychology Today*, July 1, 2014, https://www.psychologytoday.com/articles/201406/love-lust.

5. Suzanne M. Bianchi, "Family Change and Time Allocation in American Families," Focus on Workplace Flexibility, published at a conference in Washington D. C., Georgetown Law, Workplace Flexibility 2010, November 29-30, 2010, Sponsored by the Alfred P. Sloan Foundation, http://workplaceflexibility.org/images/uploads/program_papers/bianchi_-_family_change_and_time_allocation_in_american_families.pdf.

6. Bureau of Labor Statistics, "Employment Characteristics of Families Survey," news release, April 23, 2015, http://www.bls.gov/news.release/famee.nr0.htm.

7. Jim Thornton, *Chore Wars* (Newburyport, MA: Conari Press, 1997), 71.

8. Adapted from Greg Smalley, "Sharing the Load," ThrivingFamily.com, August/September 2014, http://www.thrivingfamily.com/Family/Life/For%20Him/2014/chores-and-your-marriage.aspx.

9. Jill Leviticus, "Roly Poly Bug Facts," Animals by Demand Media, accessed October 13, 2015, http://animals.mom.me/roly-poly-bug-6984.html.

10. Francis Chan and Lisa Chan, *You and Me Forever: Marriage in Light of Eternity* (San Francisco: Claire Love Publishing, 2015), 68.

11. George Eliot, *Middlemarch* (London: William Blackwood and Sons, 1907) 464.

Romance Secret #10: True Love Endures

1. IMDb, "The Last of the Mohicans (1992): Quotes," accessed October 13, 2015, http://www.imdb.com/title/tt0104691/quotes?ref_=tt_ql_3. See also "LotM—"I Will Find You," uploaded February 25, 2009, accessed October 13, 2015, https://www.youtube.com/watch?v=yoSzetoxZ34.

2. John Eldredge and Stasi Eldredge, *Love and War: Find Your Way to Something Beautiful in Your Marriage* (Colorado Springs, CO: WaterBrook, 2011), 39.

3. This list was created from my personal experience and augmented with the Holmes and Rahe Stress Scale (1967), which is a list of forty-one stressors.

4. "Adams Family Papers: Letter from Abigail Adams to John Adams, 1 October, 1775," Massachusetts Historical Society, accessed October 15, 2015, http://www.masshist.org/digitaladams/archive/doc?id=L17751001aa.

5. Linda J. Waite, Don Browning, William J. Doherty, Maggie Gallagher, Ye Luo, and Scott M. Stanley, "Does Divorce Make People Happy? Findings from a Study of Unhappy Marriages," (New York: Institute of American Values, 2002), 5, https://fhjfactcheck.files.wordpress.com/2011/10/unhappymarriages2.pdf.

6. *Love and War*, 38-39.

7. "The Last of the Mohicans: Quotes," IMDb, accessed October 13, 2015, http://www.imdb.com/title/tt0104691/quotes?ref_=tt_ql_3.

8. See Matthew 9:17, Mark 2:22, and Luke 5:37-8.

9. See Joshua 1 for encouragement to be strong and courageous.

Romance Secret #11: True Love Looks Inward

1. IMDb, "Seabiscuit (2003): Quotes," accessed August 14, 2015, http://www.imdb.com/title/tt0329575/trivia?tab=qt&ref_=tt_trv_qu.

2. Drew's Script-O-Rama, "Seabiscuit Script—Dialog Transcript," accessed August 14, 2015, http://www.script-o-rama.com/movie_scripts/s/seabiscuit-script-transcript-horse-racing.html.

3. IMDb, "Seabiscuit (2003): Synopsis," accessed August 14, 2015, http://www.imdb.com/title/tt0329575/synopsis?ref_=ttpl_pl_syn.

4. See 1 Thessalonians 3:12, Psalm 89:2, Psalm 86:15, Psalm 108:4, Psalm 86:13, Psalm 94:18, Psalm 119:64.

5. See John 7:38, Psalm 36:9, Proverbs 10:11, Proverbs 13:14, Zechariah 14:8, Jeremiah 2:13, Jeremiah 17:13, John 4:10-11, Revelation 7:17.

6. *Barnes' Notes*, s.v. Proverbs 5, http://biblehub.com/commentaries/barnes/proverbs/5.htm and Gill's Exposition, s.v. Proverbs 5, http://biblehub.com/commentaries/gill/proverbs/5.htm.

7. Gary Chapman, *The Marriage You've Always Wanted*, (Chicago: Moody, 2009), 24.

8. *Strong's New Testament Greek Lexicon*, s.v. 3670 *homologeo*.

9. The Lord's Prayer can be found in Matthew 6:9-13 and Luke 11:1-4.

10. These first nine are known as the "fruit of the Spirit" (Galatians 5:22-23).
11. Thoroughbred Greats, "Seabicuit's Race Record," accessed August 16, 2015, http://www.tbgreats.com/seabiscuit/rr.html.
12. Thom Loverro, "Seabiscuit vs War Admiral: The Horse Race that Stopped the Nation," *The Guardian* (blog), November 1, 2013, http://www.theguardian.com/sport/2013/nov/01/seabiscuit-war -admiral-horse-race-1938-pimlico.
13. IMDb, "Seabiscuit (2003): Quotes," accessed August 14, 2015, http://www.imdb.com/title/tt0329575/trivia?tab=qt&ref_=tt _trv_qu.

Romance Secret #12: True Love Fellowships

1. "LOTR—The Fellowship of the Ring—The Council of Elrond Part 2 (Extended Edition)," YouTube, posted January 10, 2015, https://www.youtube.com/watch?v=QOe_utzrsRU.
2. *Strong's New Testament Greek Lexicon*, s.v. 2842 *koinonia*.
3. Here are three resources that demonstrate that community is good for couples: Christopher R. Agnew, Timothy J. Loving, and Stephen M. Drigotas, "Substituting the Forest for the Trees: Social Networks and the Prediction of Romantic Relationship State and Fate," *Journal of Personality and Social Psychology* 81, no. 6 (December 2001): 1042-1057; Geoffrey Greif and Kathleen Holtz Deal, *Two Plus Two: Couples and Their Couple Friendships* (New York: Routledge, 2013); Sharon Jayson, "Couples Benefit from Friendships with Other Couples," *USA Today*, January 9, 2012, http:// usatoday30.usatoday.com/news/health/wellness/marriage/story /2012-01-08/Couples-benefit-from-friendships-with-other -couples/52457298/1.
4. See Acts 20:1-30, 1 Corinthians 9:19-23, Colossians 1:24-29.
5. See Acts 4:33-37, Acts 14:19-28, Acts 15:30-35.
6. Adapted from Suzanne Hadley Gosselin, "Opposite Sex Friends Beyond Marriage," March 19, 2010, Boundless (blog), https:// community.focusonthefamily.com/b/boundless/archive/2010 /03/19/opposite-sex-friends-beyond-marriage.aspx.
7. Excerpted from Plumb and Susanna Foth Aughtmon, *Need You Now* (Nashville: Shoe Publishing and Street Talk Media, 2014), 133.

More Fun Ways to Help Your Marriage Thrive

FOCUS ON THE FAMILY

FREE BONUS MATERIAL

Crazy

Little Thing

Called

Marriage

12 Date Night
Ideas &
Discussion
Guide

DR. GREG & ERIN SMALLEY

Download your free date night PDF at
www.crazylittlethingcalledmarriage.com.